THE NEW ECONOMIC DISORDER

LARRY BATES

CREATION HOUSE
BOOKS ABOUT SPIRIT-LED LIVING
ORLANDO, FLORIDA

Creation House
Strang Communications Company
600 Rinehart Road
Lake Mary, FL 32746
Fax: (407) 869-6051

Unless otherwise noted, all Scripture quotations are from the
King James Version of the Bible.

Scripture quotations marked NKJV are from the New King
James Version of the Bible. Copyright © 1979, 1980, 1982
by Thomas Nelson Inc., publishers. Used by permission.

Dedication

*This book is dedicated to the memory of and in honor of
my parents, Edward Bates and Inez Agee Bates, and the
many other godly parents around the world. I praise God
for parents who instilled godly principles and values in me
at a very early age.*

Acknowledgments

This book is the result of a collection of efforts. Heartfelt acknowledgments are due to everyone who assisted and supported me in so many ways. To Strang Communications, Creation House and its publisher John Mason, thanks for your encouragement to do this work. For editorial assistance and work on the manuscript, I am especially grateful to the editors at Creation House, Marilyn Brannan in our Colorado office and Nancy Davis in our Tennessee office.

For research assistance in many areas, I am especially indebted to Job Seese, Robert W. Lee, Charles E. Bates, Carolyn Schultz, Rose Anne Sorrels, Gordon Mitchell and all the staff at FAMC, Inc.

For both inspiration and encouragement in the area of Bible prophecy, I am grateful to Norman Franz and Kevin Van Der Westhuizen, my teammates on the prophetic seminar circuit.

And to my wife, Barbara, and my sons, Chuck and Bob, who were widowed and orphaned many times over the past several years during my travels and during periods of seclusion for writing in 1994, thanks from the bottom of my heart for your love, encouragement and understanding.

Contents

List of Illustrations

Introduction

The greatest shock of this decade is that more people are about to lose more money than in any time before in our history. But the second greatest shock will be the incredible amount of money just a relatively small group of people will make at exactly the same time.

God has promised in His Word that the wealth of the wicked is stored up for the righteous. I believe that He is raising a generation of "Josephs" to receive the end-time transfer of wealth. I believe these "Josephs" will be used of God to minister to and help prepare the bride for the Lord's return. The decade of the nineties will be exciting for those who understand what's happening and are ready and willing to be led of God.

I am not a "doom and gloomer"! I wholeheartedly believe we are standing at the threshold of a decade overflowing with opportunity, especially in finances and ministry. By understanding the "system," you can tap into that flow, and you can find yourself healthier, wealthier and wiser. A select few people have done exactly that during the last eight decades.

By now you are probably asking, "Who are these people anyway? And why does he think he can help me do the same?" Let me answer that by making what might seem to be a startling statement.

"It's All a Setup"

The new world order is marching across the entire landscape of the earth, and the initial phase of the "order's" plan is to level everybody out and make them equal...equally poor, that is, under their new economic order.

The peaks and valleys, booms and busts in the economy...all those "opportunities to profit"...are actually the result of deliberate policy actions by policy makers in the government and the Federal Reserve. Simply put, there is a small group of people in this country and around the world who have the resources and the power to determine the direction our economy will take. They can choose which investments will prosper and which will fail. That's how they transfer wealth out of your pocket, while knowing where the next profits will occur enables them to put that same money in their pockets.

Now what kind of system would permit this kind of chicanery? Easy — the kind we have. It's a discretionary monetary economy. It's called Keynesian economics. I call it the biggest Robin Hood theft ever...because it takes from the ignorant and gives to the well informed.

Wouldn't you rather be one of the informed? Wouldn't you rather know what the economic insiders are doing, take your hints from them, win the resulting profits and then use those profits as God directs? I would, and I intend to do exactly that. But before I tell you how, let me tell you who.

Confessions of a Former Insider

Remember the schoolyard taunt, "It takes one to know one"? In some ways, it's still true, but I'm not referring to childish name calling here. I'm talking about two of the most despicable, deceptive and downright dangerous groups of so-called "professionals" in this country today — two groups that already have cost you and me billions of dollars; and unless we're alert to what they plan for us next, they will cost us untold billions more.

The two groups I'm referring to are the money manipulators and their political enforcers. You may know them by the terms they prefer to use — bankers and government leaders. These are two groups that we're supposed to trust and respect — two groups that allegedly have our best interests at heart — two groups that we've been told are usually sensible, cautious, even conservative.

Baloney! I know how phony that PR is because for a while I was a member of both groups — but not anymore. Now I'm helping people like you preserve their assets and get positioned to make substantial profits by knowing how these unconvicted criminals have rigged the game for their own benefit. But before I tell you how to do that, let me tell you how I came by this knowledge.

How Could I Be So Wrong?

When I first graduated from college, I honestly believed that our political leaders were public servants. That was the reason I decided to run for public office.

I was overjoyed when, at the ripe old age of 25, I was elected to the Tennessee House of Representatives. I was even more proud and hopeful when I was elected majority floor leader in the House while still just a freshman legislator.

During my three terms in the Tennessee House of Representatives, I became chairman of the powerful banking and commerce committee. That was when my eyes were first opened to some of the devious schemes being hatched by our so-called leaders. That was also when I learned that most of what I had been taught about economics was not too reliable.

I can truthfully say my own biggest obstacle to understanding economics was my formal training in it. Now don't get me wrong; I'm still loyal to the University of Tennessee. I'm a past president of the national alumni association and a former member of its board of governors, but I can't endorse the economics education I received there.

I learned that the economy was supposed to function based on several "natural laws"...that everything happening in the markets — all the head-spinning twists and turns — were "natural phenomena" caused by all the different factors "impacting" the economy, such as supply, demand, etc. Boy, was I naive! I bought it — all of it. But now I know better.

What is happening has been happening for a reason — because the bankers and politicians planned it that way. And that's how economics really works. But there's a bright side to all of this; that is, once you understand how the economy is being operated and who's behind it, you can profit on the same scale they do — and you don't even have to start out rich to do it. I will say more about that in later chapters.

The second lesson I learned about politics was that it could be dirty — not only dirty, but downright mean. After an unsuccessful run for the United States Congress against an entrenched liberal incumbent, I left the legislature and returned to a job in what I thought was an honest industry. In fact, I deliberately chose one that seemed above petty dealings, deception and deceit. Remembering all those marvelous virtues Jimmy Stewart extolled in "It's a Wonderful Life," I became a full-time banker. Was I ever wrong…again.

Yet Another Rude Awakening

Not only did I become a full-time banker, I was chief executive officer (CEO) and majority owner of three small banks in Tennessee. We ran those banks as you would like a bank to be run. There were no third world loans or pyramiding of debt. We were careful with our depositors' money because we knew it was their money, not ours. Our bank may not have been popular with the big boys on Wall Street and at the Federal Reserve, but we treated our depositors well and made a profit for our shareholders.

Think how much better off this country would be if more banks could make that same statement today. But a funny thing happened to what had once been a staid, even stodgy profession — the swingers and wheeler-dealers started taking over, and not just in Washington or on Wall Street. It was happening right in my own state and in my own hometown. I knew the results would be disastrous, but I was just one small passenger way in the back on that particular bus. Since I couldn't stop the drivers — endorsed by the Federal Reserve and approved by the banker's association — from going over the edge, I decided to get off the bus.

More than a decade ago I sold the banks, resigned my position, and left banking. That's when I knew I needed to do something that would make a difference — something that would help the little guy use the market manipulators the way they have been using the economy to make money. Friends thought I was crazy for selling our banks, but since then thousands of banks and savings and loans have gone under. The losses are in the hundreds of billions of dollars.

I'm sorry to report that some old friends and former customers lost fortunes when their paper empires collapsed. I tried to warn colleagues and business associates about the dangerous game they were playing, but they did not listen. The truth wasn't very popular then. And in some quarters, it's still not very popular today.

The Worst Kind of Lie

I'm not writing this book to tell you that money manipulators have found the key to painless prosperity; it simply isn't true. I'm not going to claim that massive deficits don't matter...that debt can be rolled over forever...that someone will always be found to buy our bonds, T-bills and mortgages. I won't say it, because it's a lie — a lie that's being foisted on us

by government officials, central bankers, mainstream economists, a captive press and, unfortunately, by some misinformed
pastors. It's a lie that's easy to sell, because most people want to
believe it. I hope you're not one of them. I hope you agree with
Patrick Henry, one of my favorite founding fathers, who said:

> It is natural for man to indulge in the illusions of
> hope. We are apt to shut our eyes against a painful
> truth and listen to the song of that siren 'til she
> transforms us into beasts. Is this the part of wise
> men, engaged in a great and arduous struggle for
> liberty? Are we disposed to be among the number
> of those who, having eyes, see not, and having ears,
> hear not, the things which so nearly concern their
> temporal salvation? For my part, whatever anguish
> of spirit it may cost, I am willing to know the whole
> truth; to know the worst, and to provide for it.[1]

Our economy is in serious trouble. You know it and I
know it, but most people simply refuse to honestly face the
facts. Therein lies their peril and our greatest profit opportunities of the past sixty years.

Today in America we are living in a fool's paradise. We
seem to believe we've found the secret that eluded the ancient
alchemists: We believe we can slap ink on paper and somehow
it will turn to gold. The money manipulators have successfully created the illusion of prosperity through the most massive creation of debt and paper money that has ever occurred
in history. That debt bubble is about to burst; when it does,
all those loanership investments your friends, and maybe even
you, think are safe...CDs, bonds, mutual funds...will be in

deep, deep trouble. And that's just the tip of the iceberg about to ram us.

A Whole Series of Catastrophes...Each One a Golden Opportunity

I'm convinced that several irresistible forces are bearing down on us. Soon they'll hit our economy with the fury of Hurricane Andrew. When they do, all traditional assumptions and expectations will be blown to smithereens. Life as we have known it in the U.S. is about to change — and change drastically.

All of these forces are clearly visible on the horizon now. You hear about them every day. And yet, not one person in a hundred realizes the consequences these explosive forces will have on his God-given wealth. I believe not one in five hundred is taking the simple steps that would protect him from the upheaval that is sure to come. I also believe not one in a thousand has any idea of the wealth transfer that will come from this kind of upheaval.

As I have said before, an economic time bomb is set; it's ticking, and it can mean great loss or great fortune to you. Fortunately, the choice is yours.

In the following chapters, I'm going to offer you a chance to make a conscious, deliberate choice to be among those who understand the system, act on your information and profit rather than perish financially. You will learn how politicians, central bankers and other government officials manipulate the economy and transfer wealth from taxpayers' pockets to their own...and how to turn that knowledge into wealth for yourself to use as the Lord directs. But first, you need to know what's behind all this. Once you realize what's about to happen, you'll be able to act instead of being swept away with the rest.

Five Horsemen of the Apocalypse

Someday soon, people will be saying, "Didn't anyone see this coming? Why didn't someone try to warn us?" That's why I'm writing this book. Here are five powerful, dangerous and unstoppable forces that will soon hit our economy with the force of a runaway train.

Deadly Juggernaut #1: The Banking Crisis

The recent string of bank and savings and loan closings across the country has reached epidemic proportions. Remember those photographs in the media a few years ago of anxious depositors standing in line, hoping to get some of their money back? You don't see those pictures anymore, but not because the problem has gone away — in fact, it has gotten worse. The reason you don't see those photographs is that the press doesn't want to worry its readers.

Friend, when our leaders tell me not to worry, I really get scared!

How many banks and financial institutions are going to fail before this crisis is over? Nobody knows. The number may reach into the thousands, with the price tag to clean it up possibly in the hundreds of billions of dollars. Don't believe anyone who tells you the worst is behind us. Far greater havoc and far greater losses are right around the corner.

Is your bank safe? Does your bank risk money in the derivatives market? Do you know how to find out? What changes have you made in your personal portfolio and your own financial planning because of this? Most Americans would answer, "None." But as bad as the domestic situation is for our financial institutions, it's even worse when you add the third world debt crisis.

Just five Latin American countries (Mexico, Argentina, Brazil, Chile and Venezuela) owe our eleven largest international banks an amount equal to 157 percent of total stockholder equity.

Brace yourself to face a couple of very unpleasant facts:

These debts will never be paid by the countries that owe them, but *they will be paid.* How? By you and me and every taxpayer in this country. The Monetary Control Act of 1980 allows the Federal Reserve to buy such worthless foreign government debt. The Federal Reserve is even allowed to "monetize" such debt — that is, turn it into more U.S. dollars. If necessary to keep the system intact, the Federal Reserve could buy all third world debt.

In short, a new devastating banking crisis could erupt at any moment. This whole house of cards is about to collapse. When this very shaky structure begins to crash, you don't want your hard-earned assets tumbling with it, and you certainly don't want to depend on the FDIC to bail you out. You want to be on the profit side of the ledger. Later I'll tell you how, but first, let's examine another hard reality our officials wish wasn't there.

Deadly Juggernaut #2: Federal Debts and Deficits

Several years ago I warned my clients that the Gramm-Rudman Act was like trying to cover a severed artery with a band-aid. Now it's not even that good. In fact, Congress just ignores it. Over and over again, we're told by president after president, Democrat and Republican alike, that federal spending is finally coming under control. Nothing could be farther from the truth. Despite the optimistic smiles that politicians like to wear, and despite everything you might have heard about Gramm-Rudman, the deficit is going nowhere but up.

Since 1981, the federal debt has more than quadrupled. Our decade of economic expansion was bought on credit…by issuing a sea of government IOUs (T-bills and bonds) that will never be repaid.

The Grace Commission has predicted that at current spending rates, the federal budget will reach $5 trillion by the year 2000, with a federal deficit that same year at $1.3 trillion. I personally believe they have erred on the side of caution. I think the reality will be worse than that. Most Americans don't realize that the federal debt is growing at a hyperbolic rate. They are mesmerized by the paper yields offered by T-bills, certificates of deposit (CDs) and the apparent health of the stock market.

This game of financial musical chairs can't continue much longer. When it ends there will be a mad scramble out of the safe, traditional investments, but by then it will be too late. You need to get ready now. I will explain how to escape the coming storms, but first, here's another problem about to explode in our faces.

Deadly Juggernaut #3: Business and Personal Debt

Our total domestic debt is now more than $12.5 trillion. Nobody even pretends there is enough wealth in this country to pay it. It's easy to point our finger at runaway government debt as the chief threat to our economic well-being, but the truth is we are in even greater danger from the horrendous business and personal debts we have racked up. (One reason this debt is an even bigger threat is that, unlike Uncle Sam,

18

you and I aren't allowed to print the money we need to pay our bills.)

In 1980, outstanding household debt (mortgage debt and consumer installment debt) equaled 16 percent of household net worth and 72 percent of disposable personal income. By 1988, household debt rose to 20 percent of household net worth and a staggering 91 percent of disposable income. No wonder hardly anyone is paying off their charge cards anymore. Total consumer debt, excluding mortgages, is estimated at more than $800 billion.

Frightening as that amount is, business debt is much, much higher. I don't need to say anything more here about the horrendous mess our banks have created for themselves and us, but that's just part of the horrifying picture. Add to it:

- Leveraged buyouts, which have left scores of our biggest corporations owing tens of billions of dollars;
- Our farms and small business owners who are mortgaged to the hilt and still can't make ends meet; and
- The coming real estate crash, due to higher interest rates, which will decimate values of buildings and homes from one end of the country to the other.

Remember, all of this is happening at a time when the economic cycle is at a peak. Think what will happen when the coming recession or depression (which is now unavoidable) finally arrives. There are only two possible outcomes to this scenario: 1) Either there will be a massive defaulting of debt (including CDs, bonds and notes), or 2) a tremendous amount of new debt will be created to service the old. Option 1 means a deflationary collapse; option 2 means an inflationary spiral. Our bankers and politicians haven't given us much of a choice, have they? And as they say on TV, "But wait — there's more."

Deadly Juggernaut #4: Recession/Depression

It is no longer a case of will the economy hit the wall; it already has. Some parts of the country, like California, are in a recession now. In other parts, people are borrowing and buying, just as people did in the late 1920s when they thought prosperity would never end. With the relatively low interest rates of late 1993 and early 1994, many people bought more house than they could really afford; the recent rise in interest rates has them locked into property from which they probably can never recoup their money.

All across the country corporate America is reducing its workforce, including many higher paying white collar jobs. Unemployment is rising, and it's about to get worse — much worse. Many unemployed people are not even being counted in government statistics because they have given up looking for a job.

Personal bankruptcies in the last five years are at a post-depression high. Seventy billion dollars in assets were involved in business failures last year, and it's getting worse. Just a few years ago saw one of the biggest failures in U.S. retailing history — the $10 billion chain of Campeau Department Stores.

A study by the Brookings Institute says that a recession on the scale of the one we suffered in 1974 will put 10 percent of all U.S. corporations out of business. Will we repeat 1974, or even 1929? No, I'm afraid the next recession or depression will be much worse, and it will be compounded by the biggest Robin Hood theft in all of recorded history. Later on, I'll show you in detail the awesome power of the international bankers to collapse the economy without warning.

Deadly Juggernaut #5: Massive, Renewed Inflation

Nobody wants to hear the word "inflation" today, but we ignore it at our peril. This juggernaut is the most dangerous genie of all. When new clients call me to discuss the state of the world and the prospects for our economy, one of the most common questions asked is, "Larry, when will inflation return?" Friend, that is the wrong question. Inflation never left.

Let's clear up a misconception about inflation. Despite what politicians and money manipulators would like you to believe, inflation is not rising prices. That is only a symptom of inflation, just as sniffles are the symptom of a cold. Knowledgeable people are well aware that inflation is an increase in the supply of money — period. Nothing more and nothing less. The more money the Federal Reserve prints and pumps into our economy, the higher prices will be driven up.

Is the money supply being increased, and is that increase in the money supply causing prices to go up? The answer to both questions is an emphatic yes. As a consequence, we already have inflation. The only questions to be asked are, "How high will it rise? How quickly will it rise? How high is inflation today?" Well, if you listen to the government spokesmen, you will hear it's somewhere between 4 and 5 percent. But Martin Armstrong of the highly respected Princeton Economic Group says that we are already victims of double digit inflation. The true rate right now, he contends, is more than 12 percent.

Don't trust the government's inflation numbers. The government keeps changing the formula used to calculate the cost of living increases. By some strange coincidence, those items going up the fastest are frequently eliminated from the basket of goods they are measuring! For example, when in the seventies house prices were skyrocketing, the cost of houses was eliminated from the basket of goods for the CPI, and rent equivalents were substituted.

A few months ago the *Wall Street Journal* ran a survey of price increases at the grocery store. The author discovered that he was paying, on average, 39.2 percent more for items than he had a year earlier. If you don't believe this is happening, you haven't been grocery shopping lately.

No, inflation has not disappeared. I am convinced it is already much higher than the official rate of 4.4 percent, but as the circus ringmaster likes to say, "You ain't seen nothing yet."

Inflation is going to make its presence felt with a vengeance, and it's going to happen within the next few years. Most people will be shocked and dismayed. A few will already have made preparations to profit from it. As I see it, you have only two choices: To benefit from the coming monetary depreciation or to be hurt by it. Like the commercial says, "The choice is yours."

Get Ready for the Coming Storm

If just one of these juggernauts takes place, the results will be catastrophic for most people. Their traditional plans and portfolios will be decimated or worse. But I'm not worried that one of them will hit us in the next few years; I'm concerned about what happens when two, three or four strike us at once.

"It will never happen," you say. For your own sake and the

sake of your family, get your head out of the sand and look at what is really happening around you. I implore you; the storms that are about to hit will make Hurricane Andrew look like a summer breeze.

Most people will be caught totally by surprise and, as a result, many of them will be utterly devastated. They may still have dollars, but they won't have true wealth. The massive subterranean shifts that are already at work in our economy will rob them just as surely as a mugger on a dark street. But do you know what? Most of these victims won't have any idea of what happened to them.

Are We Doomed?

Absolutely not. Turn turmoil into real wealth. The coming financial Armageddon doesn't have to devastate you. If you understand what's going to happen and are smart enough (and bold enough) to position yourself on the winning side of the coming wealth exchange, you can be the wise and good steward that God intended you to be. It has happened before. A handful of financial insiders did exactly that during the Great Depression. They saw what was coming and sold their paper assets before the crash. When other people were standing in lines to get bread and soup, these shrewd investors were buying — buying farms, banks, buildings and whole companies for pennies on the dollar.

There were huge and tragic losses, but whole new fortunes were also created. Vast new empires were forged. And it's going to happen again, but this time the stakes are even higher because political freedoms and personal liberty are at stake.

One thing will decide whether you'll be one of the winners or one of the losers — knowledge. John 8:32 says, "And ye shall know the truth, and the truth shall make you free." It's not just the truth that will make you free; it's your knowledge of the truth that will make you free.

Chapter 1

UNDERSTANDING THE TIMES

B ut thou, O Daniel, shut up the words, and seal the book, even to the time of the end: many shall run to and fro, and knowledge shall be increased" (Dan. 12:4).

People today are running to and fro and knowledge is increasing, but does the church have wisdom today? What is that wisdom that is referred to in Proverbs 16 when it says, "Understanding is a wellspring of life"? The wellspring of life is perhaps the fountain of life; it is the source of our spiritual vitality. In other words, it is our training. It is the discipline that we have — the discipline in understanding the times in which we're living.

How much better is it to get wisdom than gold! and to get understanding rather to be chosen than silver! (Prov. 16:16).

Understanding is a wellspring of life unto him that hath it: but the instruction of fools is folly (Prov. 16:22).

One day I noticed a particular couple as I was addressing a crowd of people at a public gathering. After I had finished talking to the group, this couple approached me and said, "You're Larry Bates, aren't you?"

I answered, "Yes, I am."

They continued, "Well, we've never met you, but we recognized your voice from radio programs. We want you to know, first off, before we get into conversation, that we know what time it is."

That spoke volumes to me; they were telling me they understood the times. They were saying they understood the occurring sequence of events — that a new world order was at hand — that the events taking place were the same events prophesied in God's Word.

Many times when I have the occasion to address a group of people, I will often ask them to answer a few questions by raising their hands. When we're talking about economics and finances, I always ask the question, "How many watch the financial reports on television?" And a few hands are raised.

Then I ask, "Well, how many read the financial pages of the newspapers?" A few more hands are raised.

Then, I ask the loaded question, "How many of you watch the weather report?" Almost everyone raises their hands to signify that they watch the weather forecasts on a consistent basis.

Christ addresses that Himself in Luke 12:54-56:

> And he said also to the people, When ye see a cloud rise out of the west, straightway ye say, There cometh a shower; and so it is. And when ye see the south wind blow, ye say, There will be heat; and it cometh to pass. [Then He really nails us] Ye hypocrites, ye can discern the face of the sky and of the earth; but how is it that ye do not discern this time?

When we go to 2 Timothy 3:1-7, we find:

> This know also, that in the last days perilous times shall come. For men shall be lovers of their own selves, covetous, boasters, proud, blasphemers, disobedient to parents, unthankful, unholy, without natural affection, trucebreakers, false accusers, incontinent, fierce, despisers of those that are good, traitors, heady, highminded, lovers of pleasures more than lovers of God; having a form of godliness, but denying the power thereof: from such turn away. For of this sort are they which creep into houses, and lead captive silly women laden with sins, led away with divers lusts, ever learning, and never able to come to the knowledge of the truth.

I believe that we all have to agree that we are living in the last days. We are living in perilous times. Part of the American arrogance is the belief that it can't happen to us. Nothing bad can really happen to America because, after all, this is America; nothing bad has ever happened and we simply can expect nothing bad to ever happen to America.

I think we have to understand that life as we have known it in the United States is about to change, and it is about to change drastically. Why? Because of the times that we're living in.

Unfortunately, much of the apathy in our country is centered inside the church. I must say that the church simply cannot go on living in this blind, apathetic confidence of a never-ending American dream. This delusion of hope has kept us from discerning the signs and indicators of the perilous times we are in, and more importantly, those perilous times that lie ahead.

We are creatures of comfort and as such have grown accustomed to our comfort zones. We will never be moved to anything unless our comfort zones are invaded. I can tell you that, if you lack understanding and knowledge of the times, your comfort zones are about to be wrecked. Our standard of living, incredible compared to the rest of the world, and our ease of life have literally disconnected us from reality.

Just what is that reality? It may surprise some of you, but the reality is that we are at war. There is a war that is raging right here on earth, as well as a spiritual war that is being waged in the heavenlies. It is a war of world views. The kingdom of God is being viciously opposed by the kingdom of Satan. This war is real with very high stakes — the salvation of men, women, boys and girls throughout the whole world.

Tragically, many people have failed to understand that victory does not come without a fight. Let me repeat that: We cannot have victory without a fight. This is not a spectator event; you can't sit on the sidelines and watch the action in this one. This is the war of all wars; being a spectator means you will be swept away and never know what hit you. The events which are about to unfold across the landscape of this world will be more devastating and have more impact than any events we have ever seen in recorded history. That is why the Lord has instructed His people throughout His Word, about wisdom and understanding.

My son, if thou wilt receive my words, and hide my commandments with thee; so that thou incline thine ear unto wisdom, and apply thine heart to understanding; Yea, if thou criest after knowledge, and liftest up thy voice for understanding; if thou seekest her as silver, and searchest for her as for hid treasures; then shalt thou understand the fear of the Lord, and find the knowledge of God. For the Lord giveth wisdom: out of his mouth cometh knowledge and understanding. He layeth up sound wisdom for the righteous: he is a buckler to them that walk uprightly. He keepeth the paths of judgment, and preserveth the way of his saints. Then shalt thou understand righteousness, and judgment, and equity; yea, every good path. When wisdom entereth into thine heart, and knowledge is pleasant unto thy soul; discretion shall preserve thee, understanding shall keep thee: To deliver thee from the way of the evil man, from the man that speaketh froward things; who leave the paths of uprightness, to walk in the ways of darkness; who rejoice to do evil, and delight in the frowardness of the wicked; whose ways are crooked, and they froward in their paths (Prov. 2:1-15).

You need to understand that there is a master plan. This master plan has been recorded in God's Word and prophesied in His Word. The Lord is continually exhorting His people. In Revelation, throughout the second chapter, the Lord, through John the Revelator, is repeatedly saying:

He that hath an ear, let him hear what the Spirit saith unto the churches (Rev. 2:29).

What is the Lord saying to the churches today? I believe the Lord is saying through His Word that the anti-Christ system is upon us. It is a system that pits the kingdom of God in a fierce battle with the kingdom of Satan. Again, I emphasize there is a master plan recorded in the pages of the Holy Bible. This plan has also been laid out in the pages of man's works, all the way from the plains of Shinar when they were building the Tower of Babel to the United Nations complex in the landscape of New York City.

I have said for many years that the term "new world order" is merely a code word for one-world socialism, with an elite ruling class to govern the rest of us under their demonic system. The elements and phases of this new world order that we will discuss in detail later in this book are (1) the new economic order (or as the title of this book suggests, economic *disorder*), (2) the new political order and (3) the new religious order. It is my belief that the mechanism that has been set up to manage us all is a world government, an anti-Christ system, headquartered at the United Nations.

A few months ago, several of our editorial staff and I visited the headquarters of the United Nations in New York City, or as the world bureaucrats call it, "the sovereign territory of the world." When we entered the U.N. complex, we were reminded at the gate that we were leaving the territory of the United States and were now entering world soil. Our purpose was to visit and explore first-hand what these folks were up to. As we entered the gate to the United Nations, that sign stuck in my mind — that although we were still in New York City, we were now on "world soil."

The statue in front of the United Nations was a rider on a horse with a bow-like object drawn (which I believe is spoken of in the book of Revelation). A smaller statue featured a pistol with its barrel twisted into a knot. On one wall near the statue of the pistol was a quotation from the prophet Isaiah: "And they shall beat their swords into plowshares" (Is. 2:4). It was evident to me that their intent is to beat your sword and my sword into plowshares — not theirs.

As we entered the main complex of the U.N. headquarters, we could see the meditation room off to our right. Also in this area is a very prominent wall-sized, stained-glass mural depicting all of the religions of the world coming together into one. In the upper left hand corner of this mural is an image of Jesus Christ. However, in the very center of the mural is a large serpent. As our group walked down a darkened corridor toward the meditation room, we observed a large stone altar, on which a meditation light was shining. Placed in front of the altar were eleven chairs, which I believe symbolically represent what we read in Daniel 7:24:

> ...out of this kingdom are ten kings that shall arise: and another shall rise after them.

31

We then journeyed throughout the complex. While in the social and economic council chambers, our young guide, a former college professor from Germany, extolled the virtues of their grand socialist schemes.

I couldn't keep still any longer and I blurted out (intending to be facetious), "Why don't you just take everybody's money, checking accounts, savings accounts, stocks, bonds, real estate, and all their other assets and just put everything in one big pile and redistribute it to everybody in the world?"

Our guide replied, "A very good idea — it's what we are trying to do here."

Our guide went on to point out with great pride that the Vatican (Holy See) even had observer status in the U.N. General Assembly, a veiled inference that all of the religions of the world are represented through the Vatican.

At that point I asked, "Who represents Christianity?"

A person traveling in our tour group replied emphatically in answer to my question, "The Holy Father, the pope, represents Christianity!"

I'll never forget the words of my associate, Norm Franz, who said with equal emphasis, "He doesn't represent me!"

Everywhere we went in this complex the propaganda machines were extolling more power for this world body. Leading this parade of power was a press release dated December 23, 1992, from the president of the United Nations General Assembly. This press release advocated a stronger role for the United Nations world body. The statement said,

> The General Assembly of the United Nations has rightly focused its attention on the report of the Secretary General, "An Agenda for Peace," which

serves as a blueprint for the future structuring and activities of the United Nations. A strong consensus now exists to act on many issues that the report singles out as facing the United Nations.

This press release brought to mind a front page article in the *Wall Street Journal*, and I quote:

> Going into a recent meeting on the Somalia crisis, Secretary of State Lawrence Eagleberger put his arm around United Nations Chief Boutras Boutras-Ghali, calling him *effendi,* an Egyptian term for "sir." "No," said the Egyptian diplomat, "call me *pasha,*" a more exalted term meaning "lord," says a diplomat who was there.[1]

Chapter 2

GOD'S PROMISES

We must understand that none of this new world order, none of this present evil age and world order has caught God by surprise. God has spoken throughout His Word about the perilous times in which we live.

> Grace be to you and peace from God the Father, and from our Lord Jesus Christ, who gave himself for our sins, that he might deliver us from this present evil world, according to the will of God and our Father: to whom be glory for ever and ever. Amen (Gal. 1:3-5).

However, God's promises include many things. God sits in the heavens and He laughs. The psalmist David pointed this out:

> Why do the heathen rage, and the people imagine a vain thing? The kings of the earth set themselves, and the rulers take counsel together, against the Lord, and against his anointed, saying, Let us break their bands asunder, and cast away their cords from us. He that sitteth in the heavens shall laugh: the Lord shall have them in derision. Then shall he speak unto them in his wrath, and vex them in his sore displeasure. Yet have I set my king upon my holy hill of Zion. I will declare the decree: the Lord hath said unto me, Thou art my Son; this day have I begotten thee. Ask of me, and I shall give thee the heathen for thine inheritance, and the uttermost parts of the earth for thy possession (Ps. 2:1-8).

One day I happened to be on a live call-in radio talk show on a station in South Dakota. One of the callers was frustrated at the message I was putting forth. He said, quite bluntly, "Bates, what in the world does the Bible have to do with economics?"

My response to him was, "Sir, suppose you have a manufacturing plant. This manufacturing plant has a lot of intricate machinery working together in the manufacturing process. And suppose, suddenly, all of this machinery starts breaking down. What is the first thing that you do?"

After a period of silence from the caller, I answered the question myself. "The first thing you do is get the manufacturer's handbook or the operator's manual to see how this machinery was made and how to put it back together in operating order."

I want to just remind you that the Bible is the Creator's handbook. It is the Creator's operating manual. Probably the best description of God's Word and His promises was found in the introduction to a *Personal Worker's Testament* put out by Gideons International:

> The Bible contains the mind of God, the state of man, the way of salvation, the doom of sinners and the happiness of believers. Its doctrines are holy, its precepts are binding, its histories are true, and its decisions are immutable. Read it to be wise, believe it to be safe, and practice it to be holy. It contains light to direct you, food to support you, and comfort to cheer you. It is the traveler's map, the pilgrim's staff, the pilot's compass, the soldier's sword, and the Christian's charter. Here Paradise is restored, heaven opened, and the gates of hell disclosed. Christ is its grand subject, our good the design, and the glory of God its end. It should fill the memory, rule the heart, and guide the feet. Read it slowly, frequently and prayerfully. It is a mine of wealth, a Paradise of glory, and a river of pleasure. It is given you in life, will be opened at the Judgment, and will be remembered forever. It involves the highest responsibility, will reward the greatest laborer, and will condemn all who trifle with its sacred contents.[1]

With those words in mind, let's see exactly what God's promises are for the times that we're living in. Let's go directly to His Word and examine His promises.

> A good man leaveth an inheritance to his children's children, and the wealth of the sinner is laid up for the just (Prov. 13:22).
> But my God shall supply all your need according to his riches in glory by Christ Jesus (Phil. 4:19).

As we read the Word of God, we also see that He promises what will happen to those who violate His precepts.

> He that by usury and unjust gain increaseth his substance, he shall gather it for him that will pity the poor (Prov. 28:8).

God wants us to remember that He is our source. If we accept Him at His Word, He promises that He is our *El Shaddai*, not our "El Cheapo." He wants us to remember that the river of blessings is from Him. Often when that river of blessings starts to flow, the reaction of our flesh is to build a dam on the river and make a nice recreational area for ourselves behind that dam. We have to understand this is not God's best for us; He is in the business of blowing up dams. God wants us to understand that He is the source of our wealth and our strength. And how do we know that? He gives us His promise in Deuteronomy:

> But thou shalt remember the Lord thy God: for it is he that giveth thee power to get wealth, that he

may establish his covenant which he sware unto thy fathers, as it is this day. And it shall be, if thou do at all forget the Lord thy God, and walk after other gods, and serve them, and worship them, I testify against you this day that ye shall surely perish. As the nations which the Lord destroyeth before your face, so shall ye perish; because ye would not be obedient unto the voice of the Lord your God (Deut. 8:18-20).

Part of what inhibits us from understanding God's promises for us is the fact that we don't really take Him at His word. For example:

Now unto him that is able to do exceeding abundantly above all that we ask or think, according to the power that worketh in us (Eph. 3:20).

This is a powerful verse in God's Word, but how many of us really take God at His Word? We have a God who cannot lie who has given us so many promises. I suppose my favorite verse in the entire Bible is Hebrews 11:6:

But without faith it is impossible to please him: for he that cometh to God must believe that he is, and that he is a rewarder of them that diligently seek him.

In Ecclesiastes 2:26 we find:

For God giveth to a man that is good in his sight

wisdom, and knowledge, and joy: but to the sinner he giveth travail, to gather and to heap up, that he may give to him that is good before God. This also is vanity and vexation of spirit.

Another tremendous promise that God has for us is in Job 27:16-17. It says,

Though he heap up silver as the dust, and prepare raiment as the clay; he may prepare it, but the just shall put it on, and the innocent shall divide the silver.

God has also promised us in His Word that He would do nothing without first revealing His secrets to His servants the prophets. The prophets have been used throughout time by God to reveal His plan to His people. A glowing example of the signs of divine judgment upon a nation can be found in Isaiah chapter 3. The Lord, speaking through His prophet Isaiah, gave us a very vivid description and outline of the signs that we should know and the promises that God has when He is about to render judgment upon a nation. The first sign is economic chaos and shortages of the basic necessities of life.

For, behold, the Lord, the Lord of hosts, doth take away from Jerusalem and from Judah the stay and the staff, the whole stay of bread, and the whole stay of water (Is. 3:1).
When a man shall take hold of his brother of the house of his father, saying, Thou hast clothing, be thou our ruler, and let this ruin be under thy hand (Is. 3:6).

The second sign of God's hand of judgment upon a nation is a void in leadership and a very low quality of officials that govern us.

> The Lord...doth take away from Jerusalem and from Judah...the mighty man, and the man of war, the judge, and the prophet, and the prudent, and the ancient (Is. 3:1-2).

I believe that what we are seeing even today in our own country is a great vacuum of leadership and a very low level of quality in our elected officials.

The third sign that we see as a sign of divine judgment upon a nation is found in verse 4, with children ruling over a nation. We have organizations that are promoting the rule of children over adults. For example, we have the United Nations Commission on the Rights of the Child that is promoting this very thing:

> And I will give children to be their princes, and babes shall rule over them (Is. 3:4).

The fourth sign of judgment upon a nation is civil unrest and insurrection. Today we have riots in neighborhoods; we have gang wars; we have youth in rebellion; and we have the dregs of the earth rising up against the honorable things of the earth.

> And the people shall be oppressed, every one by another, and every one by his neighbour: the child shall behave himself proudly against the ancient, and the base against the honourable (Is. 3:5).

I believe that the fifth sign we will see as an indicator of God's judgment upon a nation will be the fact that things will get so bad that nobody will want to be in charge.

I was in Washington recently, walking the halls of Congress. I visited with some of the members of Congress that I had known and found an absolute pall over the place. I heard the comment, "It's no fun being in Congress anymore. We're out of money, and we can't throw money at the problem." Other statements from congressmen were, "I can't satisfy anyone anymore. Everybody is so divided, and nobody agrees on any issue."

We see this as a sign of God's judgment on a country in Isaiah 3:7, where the prophet describes a people who simply do not seize the opportunity or have the courage to lead and govern because things are in such a mess:

> In that day shall he swear, saying, I will not be an healer; for in my house is neither bread nor clothing: make me not a ruler of the people.

I believe the sixth sign of God's judgment upon a nation is the fact that they allow godless, humanistic leaders to be in charge of the nation.

> For Jerusalem is ruined, and Judah is fallen: because their tongue and their doings are against the Lord, to provoke the eyes of his glory (Is. 3:8).

It is my opinion that the seventh sign of God's judgment upon a nation is probably the most glaring of the signs present in the United States and around the world today.

> The shew of their countenance doth witness against
> them; and they declare their sin as Sodom, they
> hide it not. Woe unto their soul! for they have
> rewarded evil unto themselves (Is. 3:9).

God is expressing His hot displeasure as a sign of His
approaching judgment upon a nation because of people being
in open sin and even in sodomy — which we see promoted
from the highest offices of our own government today.

I believe the eighth sign is allowing women to rule over a
nation and permitting deceit and deception to run rampant at
the highest levels of our government.

> As for my people, children are their oppressors, and
> women rule over them. O my people, they which
> lead thee cause thee to err, and destroy the way of
> thy paths (Is. 3:12).

I believe we are seeing God beginning to lift His hand of
restraint from His divine judgment upon our nation and
around the world. Up until now, particularly in the United
States, we have enjoyed relative tranquility, much prosperity,
ease and pleasure; but we have left our first love. I believe we
are seeing these signs, proclaimed by God's prophets, of what
is about to happen as a sign of His judgment upon this
nation. It is not going to be a pleasant thing to behold. Man
has simply outsmarted himself in trying to replace God on the
throne. He has swallowed the bait on the hook that Satan has
put out — the promise that man can become God.

Probably the best book, outside of God's Word, that I have
ever read is *The Law*, written back in the 1800s by French

economist and statesman Frederic Bastiat. In the book, Bastiat
tells the story of a celebrated traveler. It goes like this:

> He [the traveler] arrived one day in the midst of a
> tribe of savages where a child had just been born. A
> crowd of soothsayers, magicians and quacks, armed
> with rings, hooks and cords surrounded the child.
> One said, "This child will never smell the perfume
> of a peace pipe unless I stretch his nostrils."
> Another said, "He will never be able to hear unless
> I draw his earlobes down to his shoulders." A third
> said, "He will never see the sunshine unless I slant
> his eyes." Another said, "He will never stand
> upright unless I bend his legs." A fifth said, "He
> will never learn to think unless I flatten his skull."
> "Stop!" cried the traveler. "What God does is well
> done. Do not claim to know more than He. God
> has given organs to this frail creature. Let them
> develop and grow strong by exercise, use, experi-
> ence and liberty."[2]

This story from this celebrated traveler is a prime example
of where we are in our thinking today. It's nothing new; it's
not going to be orderly. It is the new world order. This is the
same new world order that reared its ugly head thousands of
years ago on the plains of Shinar when they were trying to
build the tower of Babel. What we have now is just coming
forth and being dressed up in modern garb — a Babylonian
system of economics and a Babylonian system of government.

Bastiat says that we should try to exercise our God-given
liberty:

God has given to men all that is necessary for them to accomplish their destinies. He has provided a social form, as well as a human form, and the social organs of persons are so constituted that they will develop themselves harmoniously in the clean air of liberty. Away then, with quacks and organizers. Away with their rings, chains, hooks and pincers. Away with their artificial systems. Away with the whims of governmental administrators, their socialized projects, their centralization, their tariffs, their government schools, their state religions, their free credit, their bank monopolies, their regulations, their restrictions, their equalization by taxation and their pious moralizations. And now that the legislators and do-gooders have so futilely inflicted so many systems upon society, may they finally end where they should have begun. May they reject all systems and try liberty, for liberty is an acknowledgement of faith in God and His works.[3]

It is obvious then that our biggest obstacle and the greatest cause of judgment upon a nation is the fact that somehow we allow the enemy — Satan himself — to get us off course into man's devices; we either forget about God's promises or we don't take them very seriously. As a result, we lack the faith to allow God to be in control of every aspect of our lives, and our efforts become characterized more by perspiration than inspiration. That's not how God desires it to be.

Again, we are at war. It is a war of world views, and Satan has a battle plan of containment through which he plans to contain us within his evil schemes, not allowing us to experience the liberty that God has for us.

Chapter 3

BATTLE PLAN
OF CONTAINMENT

A nd ye shall know the truth, and the truth shall make you free" (John 8:32).

Most people assume that the truth is going to set them free, but a close examination of this scripture indicates that "ye shall know the truth." The truth is out there — it's God's truth — but unless you know the truth, have knowledge of the truth, you will not experience the freedom that the knowledge of the truth will give you. Satan knows this very well, and for that reason he has a battle plan of containment to keep you from understanding the truth.

In our natural condition, the truth is generally met in four phases.

In phase one, truth is met with skepticism. People are skeptical about they are told; they are skeptical as the truth is revealed. They don't understand it because it does not fit into the mold of their natural understanding.

Phase two of truth is met with ridicule. Skeptical people who have no desire to understand will generally ridicule those who have received and are accepting the truth.

In phase three, truth is met with hostility. When skepticism and ridicule have not worked, those who have absolutely no curiosity and no desire to know the truth — who are, in fact, totally blinded to the truth — will become hostile. When the truth is presented or questions are raised about the truth, they will say things like, "I never want to hear about this again," or "Don't bring that subject up again; I don't want to hear it. It's totally unbelievable. Never mention it to me again."

Truth in phase four is accepted as fact when it manifests itself.

In the areas of salvation and finance, it is too late to avoid the eternal damage by the time phase four is reached. In fact, Satan may be saying right now that you can't possibly understand economics. You can't possibly understand finances. You can't possibly understand money. He may be saying that all of this is way over your head. If it's any consolation to you, I can tell you that my biggest obstacle to understanding economics was my formal training in economics. I was not taught the truth. I was taught a lie about how the economy works.

As we approach the subject of money and economics, we must approach with a very sober and prayerful attitude; this territory is at the very heart of Satan's domain. It is an area that he has controlled for centuries, using essentially three things to compensate his followers: money, power and sex. Anything pertaining to this matter must be spiritually discerned. I draw your attention to 1 Corinthians 2:

> And I, brethren, when I came to you, came not with excellency of speech or of wisdom, declaring unto you the testimony of God. For I determined not to know any thing among you, save Jesus Christ, and him crucified. And I was with you in weakness, and in fear, and in much trembling. And my speech and my preaching was not with enticing words of man's wisdom, but in demonstration of the Spirit and of power: that your faith should not stand in the wisdom of men, but in the power of God. Howbeit we speak wisdom among them that are perfect: yet not the wisdom of this world, nor of the princes of this world, that come to nought: but we speak the wisdom of God in a mystery, even the hidden wisdom, which God ordained before the world unto our glory: which none of the princes of this world knew: for had they known it, they would not have crucified the Lord of glory. But as it is written, Eye hath not seen, nor ear heard, neither have entered into the heart of man, the things which God hath prepared for them that love him. But God hath revealed them unto us by his Spirit: for the Spirit searcheth all things, yea, the deep things of God. For what man knoweth the things of a man, save the spirit of man which is in him? even

so the things of God knoweth no man, but the Spirit of God. Now we have received, not the spirit of the world, but the spirit which is of God; that we might know the things that are freely given to us of God. Which things also we speak, not in the words which man's wisdom teacheth, but which the Holy Ghost teacheth; comparing spiritual things with spiritual. But the natural man receiveth not the things of the Spirit of God: for they are foolishness unto him: neither can he know them, because they are spiritually discerned. But he that is spiritual judgeth all things, yet he himself is judged of no man. For who hath known the mind of the Lord, that he may instruct him? But we have the mind of Christ (vv. 1-16).

I ask that you prayerfully consider what I am about to tell you. Much of this information may be new; much of it will run counter to what you have understood for many years. Some of the information may even seem too far-fetched to happen in this lifetime. That is why the spirit of God must be upon our minds, so that we may understand and know the truth and that His truth will indeed set us free. The Lord Himself tells us:

Fear them not therefore: for there is nothing covered, that shall not be revealed; and hid, that shall not be known. What I tell you in darkness, that speak ye in light: and what ye hear in the ear, that preach ye upon the housetops. And fear not them which kill the body, but are not able to kill the soul:

but rather fear him which is able to destroy both soul and body in hell (Matt. 10:26-28).

Again, there is a war of world views going on. Satan does not want what's really going on behind the scenes to be understood. He doesn't want people to understand what goes on in the inner sanctums of money, banking and politics. He desires everyone to remain ignorant and neutralized.

In fact, some pastors will not even broach the subject of money. They either don't understand it or they fear they may offend those who give to the church. Some may even subscribe to the belief — even though it is certainly not biblical — that one is more righteous if poor.

I have read the Bible from cover to cover, and I have never found anywhere in God's Word that you are more righteous if you're poor. I do not believe that is God's best for His children.

Beloved, I wish above all things that thou mayest prosper and be in health, even as thy soul prospereth (3 John 2).

Another aspect of Satan's battle plan of containment is complacency — satisfaction with the present condition. He wants you to believe you're doing the best you can, that there is nothing else greater that you can be doing, financially or otherwise. I must repeat once again that this war we're in is not a spectator sport. Victory cannot be won without a fight.

I can remember campaigning for re-election to the Tennessee House of Representatives. As I traveled to one of the rural counties that I represented, I came upon a gathering of fifteen to twenty people on the front porch of a small country store.

I did not have an opponent that year, and I was simply touching base with my constituents. As I approached the store, I was asking the people to vote for me. Of course, a politician walking into the midst of a gathering like this is certainly fair game.

From the back of the group a gentleman shouted, "Son, who's running agin' ya this time?"

I replied, "I don't have any opposition this year."

Someone from the other side of the group said, "You may not have an opponent, but you've got some opposition."

That statement has stuck in the back of my mind for many years. If we are doing anything, we're going to have opposition from the enemy. We can't have victory without a fight.

Many times people become religiously neutralized, caught up in the spirit of unity. This is not at all what the Bible says. We are to have the "unity of the Spirit" (Eph. 4:3) — that is, the Holy Spirit of the living God, not a spirit of unity that simply neutralizes us religiously or otherwise.

Organized religion is probably Satan's most effective tool in his battle plan of containment. The word religion comes from the Greek word *religio* which means "to return to bondage."[1] Religion is simply man's attempt to reach God with his own rules and regulations. In other words, if you want to join my religious group, you must follow all of my rules and regulations and be submitted to the religious order; then you are accepted.

God's plan, on the other hand, did not come with rules and regulations. His plan was to reach man through the gift of His precious Son, Jesus Christ, in whom we have liberty.

For all the law is fulfilled in one word, even in this;
Thou shalt love thy neighbour as thyself (Gal.5:14).

Religion: A Tool in Satan's Hand

As I mentioned previously, the word religion comes from the Greek word *religio* which means "to return to bondage." Man has always, at the prodding of Satan, attempted to sit on God's throne and put himself in God's place. Man has even developed great organizations with which to control people in the name of religion.

I realize this may be a very sensitive area to some people. But I have never been one to run from controversy.

I believe that the financial power of the Roman Catholic Church is one of Satan's tools in his battle plan to enslave mankind in the new world order. However, I want to make it clear that I believe it is the bureaucracy of the Roman Catholic Church that is at fault. I know many people in the Roman Catholic Church have had a salvation experience and know the Lord Jesus Christ personally as their Savior.

Man has for centuries used Christian symbols of theology, but other views of history. This schizophrenic world view is running rampant among the World Council of Churches today in a doctrine called liberation theology whereby Christian symbols are applied to theology, but a Marxist view colors the whole of history.

When we read the Bible, it is evident that Christ did not spend time trying to control people's lives by moving them out of the slums and ghettos; He simply walked those squalid streets from one end to another, trying to get the slums out of the people. He planted in them the seeds of character and integrity, not the ugly desires to claim what belonged to others. When we read Luke 12:13-15, it is obvious that Christ himself was not a socialist, even though some who claim to speak for Him today are very much socialist. Such is the case of the Roman Catholic church where throughout history attempts have been made by their hierarchy to promote a socialist gospel while maintaining a different standard for themselves. I believe this fact alone will split the Catholic church. While much of the church goes apostate, many will come out in a true relationship with Jesus Christ.

If I were to ask you what is the main industry of the Vatican (the Vatican is a nation state listed in the geographic journals as the Holy See), what would you say?

According to the *World Fact Book* compiled by the United States Central Intelligence Agency, the main industry of the Vatican is "worldwide banking and financial activities."[2] Therefore when the leaders of the Vatican and others involved in the World Council of Churches speak out on economic matters, you know the vested interest they are likely protecting.

Trimming the Plants Won't Work

Part of Satan's battle plan of containment is to keep us busy trying to tidy up a paganistic world economic and political system — in other words, continue trimming the plants or shrubs in the world's garden. However, any attempt to reform is costly, complex, frustrating and, quite frankly, impossible. We must get to the root of the problem. The Bible warns us,

> But evil men and seducers shall wax worse and
> worse, deceiving, and being deceived (2 Tim. 3:13).

The economic and social structure cannot be saved but
will ultimately be destroyed by God. But suppose the economic and social structure could be improved. That can be
done only by winning sufficient numbers of people to a sav-
ing faith in Jesus Christ. In the following chapters I will make
a strong, compelling and documented case regarding the economic system and why the Bible says what it does in Revelation 18:4 (referring to Mystery Babylon, that demonic blend
of economics, politics and religion):

> And I heard another voice from heaven, saying,
> Come out of her, my people, that ye be not partak-
> ers of her sins, and that ye receive not of her
> plagues.

I cannot say it enough: you cannot have victory without a
fight. I was especially moved by a sermon by Randel McCarty,
pastor of Cathedral of Praise Assembly of God in Cordova,
Tennessee. He said, "We must see it, say it, and seize it."

He explained that we must see our goals and dreams as
God has given them to us; many times we fail to see them
because Satan attacks our ability to see them.

He says that we must say what we believe; many times
people are afraid to say what they believe because they're not
sure of what they believe.

Finally he says we must seize it. He explains that is where
the "concerned" are separated from the "committed." Pastor
McCarty says that we must "take the authority and the power

that God intended for His church and occupy until He comes."[3]

If we are to be victorious against Satan's battle plan of containment, we must see the truth as God has outlined it for us. We must be bold enough to say what we believe and committed enough to seize the opportunity. I recall the words of Paul when he stood on Mars Hill:

> Then Paul stood in the midst of the Areopagus and said, "Men of Athens, I perceive that in all things you are very religious…Truly, these times of ignorance God overlooked, but now commands all men everywhere to repent" (Acts 17:22, 30, NKJV).

We must be able to see the truth, and the truth will set us free. We must be able and courageous enough to share the truth with those who do not understand. We must be committed enough to seize the opportunity to do battle with the satanic plan for a new world order.

Chapter 4

NEW WORLD ORDER

Nothing New and Not Orderly

We must continue to understand that the term "new world order" is nothing new, and it's not going to be orderly. It is merely a code word for one-world socialism. Its proponents espouse seemingly worthwhile goals and at times may even give lip service to the ideas of free enterprise and free markets; however, for thousands of years there have been well-laid plans which have been cultivated through secret societies and organizations that have powerfully influenced world events. The pinnacle for such plans is to bring all people and nations of the world under a one-world government. That one-world government includes a one-world economic system we call "the new economic order."

Who Benefits?

The question that thinking people should pose at the suggestion of changes of this magnitude is, "Who benefits?" Since new world order is a code word for one-world socialism, the new economic order will be a socialist economic system, and the beneficiaries of the system will not be the downtrodden masses as its proponents espouse. Rather, the beneficiaries will be the economic elite. In the late 1800s a German banker by the name of Meyer Rothschild said,

> Give me control of a nation's monetary system and I care not who writes their laws. [1]

To paraphrase what Mr. Rothschild was saying, "Let me control the heart of the system — that's money — and I couldn't care less who you send to Congress, the state legislatures or city councils, because I will have total control of your every being." Therefore, we have a system that is being designed to control the economic and social behavior of everybody.

We see this exemplified where the proponents of communism proposed their system would elevate the plight of the downtrodden masses. As we all know now, that was simply a lie; as we saw the unraveling, or supposed unraveling, of the communist system, who were the beneficiaries?

In the former Soviet Union there were approximately 250 million people. It is estimated that 2.5 million were members of the communist party, and they lived very well. The rest were simply slaves with the sole responsibility of supporting a system for the benefit of the economic and political elite.

That is precisely what the same movers and shakers in the world economic and political hierarchy want to set up on a world-wide basis — a new world order. In order to do this, they are going to have to make it a world of disorder first so that people will come to them — crying out for satisfaction of immediate, temporal desires — under a system they control totally.

Origin of Plunder

It was "in the beginning" that this whole mess about to be experienced on the economic landscape began. Early chapters of the Bible record people fighting over power and money. After getting kicked out of Paradise and the Garden of Eden because of sin, man was forced to go to work. In other words, the "free lunch" had ended.

I have been most impressed by the work of Frederic Bastiat (1801-1850), a French economist, statesman and author. He did most of his writing during the years just before and after the French Revolution. This was a period when France was rapidly moving down the road to total socialism. Mr. Bastiat, a deputy in the legislative assembly, was studying and explaining every socialist fallacy as it appeared in the public forum. He addresses in very wise words the dilemma that we now face in his book, *The Law*, when he says,

> Man can live and satisfy his wants only by ceaseless labor, by the ceaseless application of his faculties to

natural resources. This process is the origin of property, but it is also true that a man may live and satisfy his wants by seizing and consuming the products of the labor of others. This process is the origin of plunder. Now, since man is naturally inclined to avoid pain and since labor is pain in itself, it follows that men will resort to plunder whenever plunder is easier than work. History shows this quite clearly and under these conditions neither religion nor reality can stop it.[2]

If you or I were to take a gun to the local market, hold it to the clerk's head and demand they empty the cash drawer, we could go to jail under the criminal statutes of any state in this country. However, if we are elected to Congress and pass a law that empties the same cash drawer, we would probably get re-elected by the people to whom we gave the money. But stealing is stealing, regardless of the name we call it. Robbery is robbery even though it may be legalized and legitimized under the guise of law.

History Is Our Map

Alfred Fraser Tyler, a British professor in the 1800s, said,

A democracy can last as long and until a majority of the people discover they can vote themselves largess out of the public treasury. They will continue to elect the politicians promising the most with the end result being a fall of the democracy due to economic ruin and chaos.

Today in the United States more than 50 percent of the American people receive some kind of government check. Since government doesn't produce anything, it can only take by force from those who are productive and give their property to the beneficiaries of the politicians' choice. This type of system ultimately causes conflict between the classes — in other words, productive versus non-productive, or rich versus poor.

Planned Conflict

This conflict is no accident. As we have mentioned, the methods of the proponents of new world order are not orderly. They embrace the philosophy of George Wilhelm Friedrich Hegel, a German philosopher in the 1800s. Hegel theorized there is "thesis, anti-thesis, and this produces synthesis."[3]

In other words, conflict brings progress and controlled conflict brings controlled progress. This system is designed to put more and more economic control into the hands of the economic elite. This is nothing new. The early nineteenth century was the era of Hegelian mania in German universities; in later years Hegelian philosophy became the foundation of Hitlerian Nazism and Marxist Leninism. Noted economist Ludwig Von Mises said,

> Although economic planning is planned chaos, it is essential for centralized political control.

You may have heard of economist John Maynard Keynes, the architect of our present economic system — an architect of the pending economic calamity that is appearing on the horizon. In 1920, Keynes wrote a book called *The Economic Consequences of the Peace.* In that book he quotes Lenin,

> By a continuing process of inflation, government can confiscate secretly and unobserved an important part of the wealth of its citizens.[4]

He goes on to say there is no surer, no more subtle way to overturn the existing basis of society than to debauch the currency. It engages all the processes of economic law that come down on the side of destruction, and does so in a manner that not one person in a million can recognize it.

To avoid being a victim of the overturning of the existing basis of society by their debauching of the currency, you must understand the system and their methods.

Know Their Methods

We are well down the road toward this new world order because of lack of understanding. The prophet Hosea in the Bible lamented:

> My people are destroyed for lack of knowledge: because thou has rejected knowledge, I will also reject thee, that thou shalt be no priest to me: seeing thou has forgotten the law of thy God, I will also forget thy children (Hos. 4:6).

Ever since the socialists in the National Education Association and the government gained control over our children's minds, we've been rapidly losing ground in the battle for the hearts and minds of our youth. We've been giving our youngsters a bogus education for a purpose — to indoctrinate them into socialist thought and expectations, thereby reducing the chance for resistance to the implementation of the new economic order and ultimately the new world order.

The biggest obstacle to recognizing the rise of this new world order is the massive amount of disinformation coming out of the government and the media. Dissemination of disinformation is only possible when people lack true understanding; therein you find the reason for keeping this true understanding from the masses.

When truth surfaces, the methods of dealing with messengers of truth when they conflict with the new world order purposes are as follows. (I have outlined them in the previous chapter, but let me repeat them because they are important.)

1. Messengers of truth are met with skepticism.
2. Messengers of truth are met with ridicule.
3. Messengers of truth are met with hostility.
4. Truth is accepted as fact when it manifests itself.

It will be too late once the new world order is in place with its economic, political and religious orders; dissent will not be a permissible activity.

Modern Day Plunder

It has been said that money moves the world. So what is money anyway? *Webster's Dictionary* says that money is "standard pieces of gold, silver, nickel, copper, paper notes, etc., stamped by government authority and used as a medium of exchange and a measure of value."[5]

Money as we know it today has been perverted, or as John Maynard Keynes said, "debauched." Why? Because we gave monopolistic control over our monetary system to a private bank called the Federal Reserve, which is *not* federal and has doubtful reserves! Remember what Mr. Rothschild of the Rothschild banking family said,

> Give me control of a nation's monetary system and I care not who writes their laws.[6]

We have two governments in this country: the duly constituted government of the president, Congress and the judicial system; and the far more powerful government of the Federal Reserve. Money does indeed move the world, and when Congress gave control of our money system to the Federal Reserve in 1913, a powerful monster was created. The Federal Reserve determines what your car or house payments are going to be, and it determines whether you have a job.

Noted economist Milton Friedman said,

> The Federal Reserve's major function is to determine the money supply. It has the power to increase or decrease the money supply at any rate it chooses.[7]

These central bankers, or Federal Reserve officials, can create a boom in the economy, or conversely they can create a recession or depression. A prime example of this was the period prior to 1929. The Federal Reserve, at its discretion,

increased the money supply by approximately 60 percent;
then at the time of the crash, they drained the money supply.
Those people who had made commitments based on the
expectation that there would be ample money available to pay
back their obligations were now unable to do so. Congressman Louis McFadden, then chairman of the House Committee on Banking and Currency, commented,

> It [the Depression] was not accidental. It was a
> carefully contrived occurrence. The international
> bankers sought to bring about a condition of
> despair so that they might emerge as the rulers of us
> all.[8]

As a former bank CEO, I have literally created millions of
dollars out of thin air with the stroke of my pen, thanks to the
fractional reserve banking system. I then charged interest on
that which I created. If you don't pay your tithe (interest) to
the world system, the banker will take your property. You
must be aware that there are plans to consolidate all financial
control under the centralized authority of the Federal Reserve,
and ultimately a world central bank that includes banking,
brokerage and even insurance.

Many may be saying, "I can't believe that they would try
to create a world central bank." I know some are thinking that
we certainly wouldn't give our sovereignty over to a world central bank. However, the "Human Development Report," a
report released by the Social and Economic Council of the
United Nations in June of 1994, says,

> A world central bank is essential for the twenty-first

century for sound macro-economic management for global financial stability and for assisting the economic expansion of the poor nations.

They go on to say,

It will take some time and probably some international financial crisis before a full-scale world central bank can be created.[9]

I am convinced they will create the international financial crisis in order that they can move in with their power structure. It's inevitable. No, I'm not a "doom-and-gloomer." Quite frankly, I'm excited about the future, but I'm excited for those who understand the system and are trying to raise their level of understanding in order to take steps to protect themselves from the effects of the coming economic collapse. We should be asking, "Collapse for whom?"

As I outlined in the introduction, in the coming few years you'll see more people lose more money than at any time before in our history. Yet at exactly the same time, a few people will forge new financial empires from the wealth that will be transferred to them. Even during economic collapse, wealth is not destroyed except for the property destroyed by civil unrest. Wealth is merely transferred.

Let's give an example. Suppose a farmer has a $1 million farming operation that includes all his land, his homestead, his buildings, his livestock and equipment. This farmer owes $500,000 on his $1 million valued operation. When economic hard times come and he can no longer make the payments on that $500,000 debt (or maybe the banker decides to arbitrarily call the loan since the farmer can no longer make the payments and he doesn't have the cash to pay off the loan), his operation is sold on the courthouse steps.

So what happens next? In all probability, someone will come in — the bank perhaps, or another individual — and bid $500,000 — the exact amount owed and exactly the amount required in this scenario to purchase the whole operation. Everything is still there — the land, the homestead, the buildings, the livestock and the equipment — the only thing that has changed is ownership. The wealth has been transferred.

Who Are These People?

If you are neither on welfare nor part of the economic elite (multi-millionaire or billionaire status), you are a target. Even if you have a few million you are a target of the new world order operatives. Without economic power, there can be little or no political power; if you're busy trying to dig out of the economic ashes, you won't be a political threat to the purveyors of this tyranny.

We can expect a drastic drop in the standard of living for the unsuspecting masses as the new economic order, or disorder, unfolds. The beginning of this period of economic disorder is not by accident, but clearly by design. For several centuries, plans have been carefully laid by the elitists to achieve for themselves both economic and political power, which go hand in hand.

Some people will be shocked by what I'm about to reveal. Others are well aware of it. In the United States, many non-profit foundations have been about the business of creating a new world order. In other words, leveling everybody out and making everybody equal — equally poor — except for the ruling classes. Rowan Gaither, president of the Ford Foundation, said:

> Most of us here were at one time or another active in either the OSS (Office of Strategic Services), the State Department or the European Economic Administration. During those times, and without exception, we operated under directives issued by the White House: the substance of which was to the effect that we should make every effort to so alter life in the United States as to make possible a comfortable merger with the Soviet Union. We are continuing to be guided by just such directives.[10]

In practical terms this means, as Mr. Gaither points out, that we must lower our standard of living and raise theirs. Again, socialism makes everybody (the masses) equal — equally poor.

Now who do you suppose Mr. Gaither was speaking for? If you review the studies, the documents and the historical references to the attempts to enslave this country into a new world order, you will find that there are two organizations that are at the forefront of the political and economic changes we are experiencing in America.

The first organization is the Council on Foreign Relations, the political arm of the establishment elite.

The second organization is the Trilateral Commission, the economic arm of the establishment elite. I want to say at the outset that all of the people involved in these two organizations are not bad people. They simply do things for the wrong reasons.

Antony C. Sutton, in his book *America's Secret Establishment*, says:

> However, there is a group within the Council on Foreign Relations which belongs to a secret society sworn to secrecy which more or less controls the CFR. CFR meetings are used for their own purposes: i.e., to push out ideas, to weight up people who might be useful, to use meetings as a forum for discussion.[11]

Since its founding in 1921, the Council on Foreign Relations has found its members involved in high levels of government, banking, commerce, trade and the media. Virtually every key policy-making post in the U.S. Government has been filled by a member of the Council on Foreign Relations or the more elitist organization, the Trilateral Commission.

The Trilateral Commission was founded in 1973 by David Rockefeller with a membership between two hundred and three hundred worldwide, of whom a little over one hundred are American. Its activities and its members' activities can be found primarily in the area of economic and monetary control around the world. It derives its name from "tri," meaning three. Its members come from three areas of the world: North America, Western Europe and Japan.

What's so significant about that? Approximately 95 percent of the world's capital, or wealth, comes from these three regions of the world. You will find their members ingrained in government, academia, banking, commerce, manufacturing, military and even the media.

The more elite of the elitist groups are well schooled in the goals of their particular order. They use their schooling in Hegelian theory — conflict brings progress, but controlled conflict brings controlled progress — to bring about their political and economic objectives. You will see their methods used throughout history in conflict after conflict because, more often than not, these same people have been on both sides of every major conflict in modern history.

Examples of Conflict

It is well documented that both sides of World War II were financed by New York bankers. The goal — to bring about the initial stages of a "one world" socialist system. You see, out of war and revolution come opportunities to profit. Conflict can be used by corporations who supply goods and services to the people involved in a conflict.

The weapons trade has been big business, and the more wars are going on throughout the world the more business booms for the weapons trade. When peace comes about, their business slacks off.

The same applies to bankers who finance wars, regardless of which side they are on. One such company is Standard Oil Company. In reading Dr. Antony Sutton's book, *America's Secret Establishment*, I saw a copy of a letter that was dated-stamped by the War Department July 17, 1941. Its subject was Standard Oil Company of New Jersey with ships operating under Panamanian registry. The letter is as follows:

To A.C. of S., G-2 War Department, Washington, DC

1. A report has been received from Cleveland, OH in which it is stated that the source of this

information is unquestionable, to the effect that the Standard Oil Company of New Jersey now ships under Panamanian registry transporting oil (fuel) from Aruba, Dutch West Indies, to Teneriffe, Canary Islands, and is apparently diverting about 20 percent of this fuel to the present German government.

2. About six of the ships operating on this route are reputed to be manned mainly by Nazi officers. Seamen have reported the information that they have seen submarines in the immediate vicinity of the Canary Islands and have learned that these submarines are refueling there. The informant also stated that the Standard Oil Company has not lost any ships to date by torpedoing as have other companies whose ships operate to other ports.

Signed for the A.C. of S., G-2
Charles A. Burrows
Major, Military Intelligence Assistant
A.C. of S., G-2[12]

Some friends of mine who who were helicopter pilots operating gun ships during the Vietnam War reported the same scenarios, where tanker trucks from U.S.-based companies would travel the highways to refuel the enemy in the north (North Vietnam) and had protective covering by orders of Washington. Once again, we see examples of the Hegelian philosophy that conflict brings progress, but controlled conflict brings controlled progress.

Another example is Operation Desert Storm. I was

shocked one evening to watch on the Cable News Network a report that our own ambassador to Baghdad, April Glaspie, had made a visit to President Saddam Hussein of Iraq. According to the transcript Ms. Glaspie told Saddam Hussein,

> If you go into Kuwait, we will consider it an Arab-to-Arab problem as we have no mutual defense treaty with Kuwait.[13]

This was at a time when Saddam Hussein had all of his tanks lined up on the border of Kuwait; this was merely the green light he needed to go in and take the Kuwait territory which he had coveted for quite some time.

After we saw the atrocities beamed across the world by satellite when Saddam Hussein's forces invaded Kuwait, we saw a very indignant president of the United States, a very indignant John Major of the United Kingdom, and a very indignant Francoise Mitterand of France all come on television that evening saying, in orchestrated sequence, that we must come together in a "new world order in order to stop a tyrant like Saddem Hussein."

What is interesting about this is that during the ten years prior to Operation Desert Storm, the United States and its allies had given Saddem Hussein more than $50 billion in loans, credits, military hardware and direct aid. In other words, we created the thesis, and we provided the anti-thesis, so it would result in the synthesis. So what was the synthesis?

The synthesis was a new world order. The United Nations had been discredited and had fallen into deep disrepute. This was a carefully planned event to rescue the United Nations and use it as a world forum, the premier mechanism for moving us into a new world order. There are carefully laid plans for the implementation of the new world order, and we are in the midst of the early stages of implementation at this time.

Chapter 5

IMPLEMENTATION OF THE NEW WORLD ORDER

I have spent much of my adult life observing and studying and researching this thing called the new world order. I am convinced that the economic and political elite and their establishment lackeys are well on their way to the full implementation of their plans and goals.

I believe that their plan involves a three-phase implementation for a new world order, or one-world socialist economic, political and religious system. I believe this three-phase plan will be: phase one, the new economic order; phase two, the new political order; and phase three, the new religious order.

Time is running short as we are experiencing economic

problems never before seen in most of our lifetimes. As they say, "You ain't seen nothin' yet."

Phase one of the new world order, the new economic order (or the new "disorder") probably will be the most peaceful of all phases, It will be much like putting the frog into warm water and gradually turning up the heat. Most people won't realize what is happening until they are cooked.

I believe that every effort is being made to hold things together until the necessary infrastructure or apparatus has been put into place. These efforts are primarily through Executive Orders and circumvention of the United States Constitution through the use of instruments such as the Crime Control Act of 1994. The *United Nations Commission on the Rights of the Child*, the Social and Economic Council Report involving their economic goals, and the president of the Security Council's report involving the implementation of a one-world army under United Nations command are also being used.

Shortly after that, expect economic forces from every sector to hit with the force of a runaway train. I said in a previous paragraph it will be peaceful; it will be peaceful until the time of absolute economic devastation.

People won't know what hit them. Those who once thought of themselves as wealthy will suddenly realize their holdings aren't worth much anymore. Others, who were not as wealthy, will be absolutely devastated financially and relegated to a life of working in a socialist setting...they pretend to pay you and you pretend to work. In this system, everybody loses except the elite at the top.

Out of the economic ashes will come an enormous outcry from a people devastated by encomic chaos, begging for government-sponsored aid. In return, they'll surrender their political freedoms and phase two, the new political order, will be ushered in.

Right now, the framework is being laid and designed for the full implementation of the new political order. This process is now well under way, with institutions of American culture, traditions and morality under major assault. In fact, our founding fathers wouldn't even recognize the America of the 90s as something they had anything to do with. In my lifetime, I've seen the following major changes in what we once knew as America:

1. There has been a massive accumulation of more than $12.5 trillion of domestic debt, of which almost $5 trillion is owed by the government.

2. Sodomites are parading all across the country and getting a blessing for their deviant lifestyle directly from the occupant of the Oval Office.

3. Government is publishing and distributing so-called sex and AIDS education material so graphic that no newspaper will dare print the contents but will criticize a public official who confiscates the material before it reaches the hands of innocent children. Such was the case when Colorado State Senator Bob Schaffer confiscated this material from the lobby of the state capitol in Denver.

4. The taking of human life by abortion is not only condoned but is defended and paid for with taxpayer funds.

5. The Secretary of Health and Human Services is proclaimed a lesbian by lesbian and gay leaders at their march on Washington.

6. Christians are under attack for involvement in political affairs and for any religious expression that is not deemed "politically correct" by the self-styled thought police.

7. The voters in America have elected a president who has admitted using drugs, having extra-marital affairs, dodging the draft, collaborating with the enemy and who openly promotes homosexuality. Either the American people don't understand his behavior or they don't care. After all, "It's the economy, stupid."[1]

8. The thought police have intimidated pastors and church leaders to accept and preach a secular humanist social gospel to tickle the itching ears of congregations that have become all too consumed in materialism, the lust of the eyes and the lust of the flesh. Many do not realize they are teaching and preaching an apostasy and are simply overcome by the fear of man.

All these things have not happened by accident, but are the result of plans and deliberate action on the part of those forces that are moving us rapidly toward their goal of a new world order. The tearing down of institutions, moral values and traditions are a must in order to eliminate any resistance to their carefully crafted plans. This plan to move us into a new political order is nothing new and it will not be orderly. We must get ready for planned chaos.

Many credible writers and publishers are drawing an ominous parallel between what happened in the 1930s in Nazi Germany and what is happening in America today. One prominent writer, Donald McAlvany, notes some of the emerging parallels.[2]

1) Preoccupation with death (abortion and euthanasia were rampant in Germany in the 1920s and 1930s). 2) Thousands of laws and regulations were passed (more than 65,000 pages of new rules

and laws were added to the U.S. Federal Register in 1992). 3) There was an occultic dimension to the Third Reich (Hitler's movement was not just a political movement; it was also a supernatural occultic movement that was in strong opposition to Bible-based Christianity and orthodox Judaism.) 4) A preoccupation with animal rights (there is an ominous parallel between animal rights legislation in the Third Reich and the Endangered Species Act in America). 5) Ignoring the Constitution (our presidents and courts, by executive order and judicial decree, are showing a growing contempt for rule of law). 6) Rejection of their heritage (government schools and publishers are erasing the old history and replacing it with a brand new, Socialist history). 7) Hitler used homosexuals, drug addicts and criminal elements to destabilize the country and advance the Nazi political machine (in America today, the government is forcing homosexuals and gangs onto the American landscape as destabilizing agents).[3]

The previous parallels between Nazi Germany and America today can be traced back to Adam Weishaupt's *Illuminati Protocols* and even to the Tower of Babel on the plains of Shinar (Gen. 11:1-4).

In Psalm 64:5-6, we read,

They encourage themselves in an evil matter: they commune of laying snares privily; they say, Who shall see them? They search out iniquities; they accomplish a diligent search: both the inward thought of every one of them, and the heart, is deep.

Their Modern Plan

Part of the American arrogance is the belief that it can't happen to us. It's happening, and it's happening faster than most people realize. We're having so many more illegal seizures and forfeitures of property by out-of-control government agencies against innocent citizens that the KGB's operations of the past several decades would pale in comparison.

The Federal Emergency Management Agency (FEMA) has been given the power to control the economic and social behavior of everyone during a declared emergency. It makes no difference that the crisis was precipitated by the government itself; this self-styled authority has come about by the issuance of unconstitutional Executive Orders by various presidents over the years. Lest you have doubts, the following Executive Orders have been issued within the last ten years:

- Executive Order 10995 — Take over all communication media
- Executive Order 10997 — Take over all electric power, petroleum, gas, fuels and minerals
- Executive Order 10998 — Take over all food resources and farms
- Executive Order 10999 — Take over all methods of transportation, highways and seaports
- Executive Order 11000 — Mobilization of civilians and work forces under governmental supervision

- Executive Order 11001 — Take over all health, welfare and educational functions
- Executive Order 11002 — The Postmaster General will operate a nationwide registration of all persons
- Executive Order 11003 — Take over all airports and aircraft
- Executive Order 11004 — Take over housing and finance authorities to relocate communities, to build new housing with public funds, designate areas to be abandoned as unsafe, establish new locations for populations
- Executive Order 11005 — Take over all railroads, inland waterways, and public storage facilities
- Executive Order 11051 — Designate responsibilities of Office of Emergency Preparedness. Give authorization to put all other Executive Orders in effect in times of increased international tension or economic or financial crisis.[4]

When you examine the caption of Executive Order 10051, the authorization is given to implement "all other Executive Orders...in times of...economic or financial crisis." During a period of economic collapse the new political order will be implemented instantly by the above Executive Orders, plus many others already in place. Did they miss anything?

Dealing With the Resistance

The greatest obstacle to this unconstitutional, self-styled, Satan-inspired, totalitarian government of the new world order will be true, Bible-believing Christians who will be branded as cultists, fanatics or dangerous fundamentalists. In the April 21, 1994, edition of *USA Today*, an article entitled "Experts Weigh How to Deal With Cults in the Future" pointed out that, "There is a rise in 'fanaticism' all across the world. Today, the groups (cults) tend to believe the Bible predicts the end of the world is near." Quoting author Paul Boyer, the article revealed, "In the past couple of decades, we've had a sharp upsurge of interest in Bible prophecy."

Like the Nazis in Germany and the Communists in Russia, the establishment liberals and conservatives in the United States share a common premise — the rejection of the supreme authority of the almighty God of the Bible. Writing in the *Colorado Christian News*, editor Joann Bruso aptly states, "This new definition for 'religious fanatics' includes every evangelical, Pentecostal and Bible-believing Christian. It's time for America to wake up."[5]

We must continue to be vigilant in understanding the plans of those who would seek to enslave us and our families, and to make plans how to deal with their methods and the events as they unfold. In the next chapter, we'll explore how they use one of their greatest weapons in capturing the hearts and minds of the people they wish to control.

Chapter 6

AGE OF DISINFORMATION

We are living in the age of the big lie. Politicians, government bureaucrats, central bankers, Wall Street, educational leaders, academicians and even the media lie on a continual and systematic basis.

Webster's Dictionary defines "information" and the prefix "dis" as follows,

> Information: an informing or being informed, especially a telling or being told of something; something told, news, intelligence.

Dis: (prefix): a way, a part, deprived of, expelled from; caused to be the opposite of.[1]

Disinformation, therefore, means to do the opposite of communicating or receiving knowledge or intelligence. The practice of disinformation probably has been more widely used among government intelligence agencies than any other single group. This is done to confuse and deceive people and governments in order to accomplish specific goals and purposes.

More recently the practice of disinformation has become standard operating procedure at the highest levels of government and among central bankers around the world. I have even detected the use of disinformation by some of the largest banks and brokerage houses in the United States.

Purpose of Disinformation

The most common purpose of disinformation is to spread false information or intelligence in order to achieve one's goals and purposes.

A former KGB agent assigned to the disinformation section, which was the "active measures" arm of the Soviet KGB, stated that they budgeted in the neighborhood of $200 million annually for disinformation directed to the United States. Their stated objective was world domination under communism, and their purpose was the destruction of western civilization.

In the United States the purpose of disinformation varies widely; its magnitude is directly proportional to the desire to achieve certain goals by high government officials and even members of Congress.

Disinformation also exists within the private sector. Those who engage in the practice are attempting to transfer power and wealth away from you to themselves and their associates.

Monetary System Encourages Disinformation

Since 1913 when Congress gave the Federal Reserve system a monopoly on the creation of money, this country has existed as a discretionary monetary economy. At the discretion of the policy makers, interest rates are set by the arbitrary expansion or contraction of the paper money supply; this effectively determines what most people's house payments or car payments will be, and whether they will even have jobs.

Monetary policy makers have used disinformation over the years to maintain their monopoly and control of the economy by making the system appear complex and impossible to understand. This system has evolved into the greatest Robin Hood theft of all time...it takes from the ignorant and gives to the well-informed, who have acted on their information and understanding of the system.

Examples of Disinformation at The Federal Reserve

Disinformation — On Wednesday, July 20, 1994, before the Banking Committee of the United States Senate, Federal Reserve Board Chairman Alan Greenspan said,

It is an open question whether our actions to date have been sufficient to head off inflationary pressures and thus maintain favorable trends in the economy.

When asked by a member of the committee whether an inflation rate of 3 to 4 percent was acceptable, Greenspan answered,

> Although that pace of inflation was not a cause for alarm, the risk is that inflation sneaks up on you.

Information — Inflation does not sneak up on Mr. Greenspan or any other Federal Reserve governor, because they make the decision to inflate the money supply in the first place to accomplish their purposes. Their concern is motivated when others understand what they are doing and the wealth transfer becomes more noticeable as the inflation figures go higher.

Disinformation — On April 5, 1991, Federal Reserve Board Governor Wayne Angell said they would continue to manage money supply growth to avoid sharp swings in prices.

> I am not proposing a gold standard nor a commodity standard, but that the Fed alter the growth path of the money stock so as to lean against the winds which are reflected in commodity prices as well as exchange rates.[2]

Information — What Mr. Angell is not telling us is that the Federal Reserve (a private bank) is already on a gold standard, but it is not for our benefit — it is for the benefit of the Federal Reserve. The Federal Reserve Board hopes that under the influence of their continued disinformation you will always accept the "psychological money" in the form of Federal Reserve notes that almost everyone presently accepts as money.

Disinformation — Federal Reserve Board Chairman Alan Greenspan said there were some benefits from the October 1987 stock market crash because it eased speculative pressure. "We're looking more normal now," he said. "We're not 'teetering on the edge' of new market problems," he stated in testimony before the House Banking Committee.[3]

Information — Benefits for whom? Mr. Greenspan fails to say that it was the Federal Reserve, by its policy actions, that deliberately precipitated the October 1987 crash.

The Federal Reserve was in a box on what to do and how to control damage to the economy by inflation, how to rally a sagging bond market, and how to finance the nation's budget deficit. During the early 1980s, then Federal Reserve Board Chairman Paul Volcker kept the dollar artificially high by keeping real interest rates (market rate minus inflation) artificially high to attract foreigners to buy our debt and thereby temporarily export our inflation. Those foreign-held dollars found their way into the U.S. stock market where the inflation manifested itself.

In September of 1987, I recommended to my clients and subscribers that they take their stock market profits and run, as the Federal Reserve was simply out of choices. The Federal Reserve Board's only option was to crash the market to achieve their purposes, avoid the collapse of the dollar, and try to rally the bond market.

The scenario went like this: Many primary bond dealers were getting battered by declining bond prices on large holdings of bond inventories in their warehouses. But how do you rally a bond market? By lowering interest rates. But how do you lower interest rates without collapsing the dollar, which is already under intense market pressure? The answer is to raise interest rates and create a crisis by collapsing the smallest of those markets (stock market). Then, you rush to aid the system by promising, as Greenspan did, to "provide all the liquidity the system needs to remain afloat."[4]

You lower the interest rates in the meantime to rally the bond market (to bail out the primary bond dealers) and the dollar doesn't crash, because everyone is "herded" to the relative safety of the dollar and U.S. Treasury issues, creating a temporary demand for dollars and bonds.

Wealth was not destroyed by the market crash as some have suggested. Wealth merely changed ownership. Wealth was transferred from those who didn't understand the system to the well-informed who had acted in time.

Disinformation — While still in the White House briefing room, just after his nomination by President Reagan to be Federal Reserve Board chairman, Alan Greenspan declared that the dollar had fallen far enough and would be stable and on the rise.

Information — Just five days earlier, Mr. Greenspan stated in a public meeting that "the dollar must fall drastically if we are to correct the trade imbalances."[5]

In the secretive world of monetary policy making, central bankers deliberately use obscure and arcane language in order to keep the financial market guessing. That is why you must understand the system if you are to survive and prosper in the coming months.

The Government Connection

Our founding fathers, with divine wisdom, gave us a constitutional form of government called a republic — not a democracy, as many would suggest. Granted, we have abdicated many of the principles laid down in the charter of this republic and have moved rapidly toward a social democracy.

Why did our founding fathers give us a republic and not a democracy? Well, they knew that a republic was designed to be a lasting and permanent form of government. That is because certain inalienable rights granted by the Creator (life, liberty and property) would be protected by law; therefore, government was simply man's agent for the protection of God's gifts. These early statesmen also knew that a democracy was a temporary and transitional form of government on the way to total government or totalitarianism.

It certainly doesn't take a genius to see how far down the road to economic ruin we have come. Listen to the rhetoric of certain political candidates who tell you of all the programs and things they are going to do for you. But these same candidates fail to tell you what it's going to cost. That is disinformation at the highest level of government.

Government has simply evolved into one big circus with a multitude of stars each striving to be the main attraction and some aspiring to be the ring master. As in a circus, we often get distracted from the main attraction and, more often than not, we lose touch with reality. Unfortunately, this evolution of government into a circus-like atmosphere has not made our attendance or financial support (taxes) any less mandatory. We are required through taxation to support each of the acts regardless of their worth, efficiency or threat to our liberties.

The one factor that causes disinformation to flourish at all levels of government is the "fatal tendency of mankind," described by Frederic Bastiat in his book, *The Law*:

> Self-preservation and self-development are common aspirations among all people, and if everyone enjoyed the unrestricted use of his faculties and the free disposition of the fruits of his labor, social progress would be ceaseless, uninterrupted and unfailing. But there is another tendency that is common among people: When they can, they wish to live and prosper at the expense of others. This is no rash accusation, nor does it come from a gloomy and uncharitable spirit. The annals of history bear witness to the truth of it: the incessant wars, mass migrations, religious persecutions, universal slavery, dishonesty in commerce and monopolies. This fatal desire has its origins in the very nature of man — in that primitive, universal, insuppressable instinct that entails him to satisfy his desires with the least possible pain.[6]

When we look at God's plan, we see that man can live and satisfy those wants through labor. That is the application of God-given faculties to the natural resources, in the midst of which He has placed us. However, in man's quest to avoid pain, he has simply resorted to plundering his fellow man. Bastiat asked the question:

> When, then, does plunder stop? It stops when it becomes more painful and more dangerous than labor.[7]

87

It is evident that the true purpose of law and government is to stop the fatal tendency to plunder rather than work. The force of law should be to protect property and punish plunder. However, we entrust men to make laws with the sanction of the majority, and as a result we have allowed the law to be our instrument of plunder.

When I was a young legislator one of my constituents, a very wise person, told me one day, "Larry, those people that are running for public office are running for either one of two reasons: (1) they want to stop the plunder; or, (2) they want to participate in it."

We must ask the question, "Why, then, do the people allow the scenario of legalized plunder to exist?" The answer is because they primarily lack knowledge and information on how the system works and how to protect themselves. Lack of discernment regarding your financial assets will place you on the losing side of the Robin Hood game that takes from the ignorant and gives to the well-informed.

Examples of Disinformation From Government

Disinformation — The Securities and Exchange Commission (SEC), in the wake of the October 19, 1987 stock market crash, sent up trial balloons to ascertain the possibility of passing legislation to grant the SEC greatly broadened emergency powers to avoid another stock market crash. They were seeking the power, subject to presidential veto, to shut down the markets for up to twenty-four hours.

Information — Witness the example of the Hong Kong Stock Exchange. After closing for the week of October 19, the market declined almost 50 percent upon re-opening. The fact is that truly free markets don't produce chaos, but produce what economist Freidrich Hayek calls "spontaneous order." Former U.S. Secretary of Agriculture Earl Butz told me one day, "If you guarantee any sector of society against failure, the best you can hope for from that sector is mediocrity."

The SEC, in order to keep the average investor attracted to investing in their monopoly game, is simply trying to give the appearance that it is safe to invest in their markets. In doing so, they grossly overlook all of the economic factors that are the driving forces behind any market.

Remember that, in the secretive world of monetary policy making, governments and central banks deliberately use arcane language in order to keep financial markets guessing. You must understand their system and use discernment if you are to prosper in this age of disinformation.

Your Connection

Let me say again that the purpose of disinformation is to spread false or misleading information and intelligence to achieve one's goals. This usually translates into separating you from your monetary assets and other products of your labor.

Recently banks, brokerage houses and other financial intermediaries have spread disinformation as the volatility of markets and the magnitude of wealth transfer has grown. The disinformation directly affecting the average person involves property and plunder. The plunder is motivated by either stupid greed or false philanthropy.

In recent years, the most useful means of plunder has been the skillful use of the media and the force of law through the control of the legislator. In other words, stealing has occurred under the cover of law. This is done for the benefit of those who control the legislator.

Right here in the United States we have bred a generation of what I call corporate wimps who run to Washington for legislation or regulation to achieve what they could not otherwise achieve in the market place. They also use the media to spread disinformation for their own purposes.

Disinformation — In early 1988 I recall seeing a four-page advertising spread by a major brokerage house, widely announcing in the major newspapers across the country a multi-million dollar media campaign: "Where we stand on treasury bonds." They proclaimed that inflation was under control and that interest rates had peaked out and would go much lower. Their categorical recommendation was to buy.

Information — This firm either did not know what they were doing — or they did. A major drop in interest rates would put intense downside pressure on the dollar and upside pressure on inflation, which would then cause upward pressure on interest rates.

In the few short years following 1988 when those "buy bonds" ads were running, the Treasury's 30-year long bond went down in price from around 106 to eighty-three, and yields rose as high as 9.2 percent. If the buyers of those February 1988 treasury bonds had decided to sell shortly after they had purchased them, they would have lost approximately 7 to 8 percent of their principal.

Let's go back to 1993. In October, 1993 interest rates hit the lowest that they had been in many years. Many people were rushing to buy long-term government bonds at those interest rates. They were encouraged by those same brokerage houses to buy bonds for the long term. Then in July, 1994 those same bonds that were bought for 100 cents on the dollar brought about eighty-seven cents on the dollar...and it will get worse.

Because of our twin deficits (trade and budget), any drop in long-term interest rates will be a temporary aberration. One should use these dips in interest rates (price rise in bonds) to unload long-term issues. Remember, interest (the time-priced differential for the use of money) has two factors affecting the rate: risk premium (whether you will get your money back or not) and inflation premium (what will be the purchasing power of your return dollars at a future date). The current state of the economy argues convincingly for higher long-term interest rates.

Why, then, the recommendation from a major brokerage house, who is also primarily a bond dealer, for you to buy long-term bonds? Was their warehouse so full of bond inventory that they needed to unload on someone else, or did they just not understand the state of the economy? That doesn't really matter as long as you are informed and have a genuine understanding of how the economy game works. You will be able to avoid the Robin Hood scenario that takes wealth from the ignorant and transfers it to the well-informed.

Disinformation — The Treasury Department says that from April through June of 1994 the government "took in $602 million more than it spent." They cited a combination of strong economic growth, higher taxes, spending restraint and the annual payment of income taxes before the April 15 deadline as having produced the surplus. They also said that the last quarterly surplus before that was April through June of 1989, when the government took in $23 million more than it spent thanks to spending restraints and a peaking economy.

Information — For the first time in five years, the federal government has run a quarterly budget surplus. It is true that the government took in $602 million more than it spent. But where did it get the money? It still added $7.7 million to the national debt. They simply borrowed the money and counted this borrowed money as cash flow in the treasury statement to get us to believe that we really had a surplus for that period of time.

Writing in the July 25, 1994, issue of *U.S.A. Today*, Mark Memmot said:

> The government borrowed another $7.7 million from the public last quarter and did so to keep from upsetting financial markets which could push already rising interest rates even higher. "The markets want to see a stable pattern of borrowing," says Michael Englund, chief economist at MMS International. "They don't want the government to suddenly disappear."

Also, Memmot says they borrowed to add cash to their coffers for payment of future bills.

> "In a sense, the government borrowed to add cash to its checking account," Englund says. "In June alone, the Treasury says the government added $24 billion in operating cash."[8]

Disinformation — White House Counsel Lloyd Cutler, previewing administration tactics for the congressional hearings on Whitewater, said on CBS's "Face the Nation" that his internal review of White House actions found nothing more than "regrettable errors of judgment."[9]

Information — The prisons of our country are filled with people whose actions were nothing more than "regrettable errors of judgment." What we have here is the political elite observing a double standard that says to the American people, "Some people are more equal than others." And as they say, "The list goes on."

The disinformation process encompasses all aspects of society; history shows that we in the United States don't have a monopoly on ignorance.

What's the answer? Our level of understanding must be raised, because the only way we can avoid being a victim of the new economic disorder is to have a greater degree of enlightenment than most now possess. The prophet Hosea lamented in Hosea 4:6, "My people are destroyed for lack of knowledge." That is straight from the Creator's handbook.

Where are we in our process of moving from an open society to a closed society? How does the disinformation process work?

I was fortunate to have the opportunity to debrief a former KGB agent who defected to the United States. He provided me with charts 1 and 2 that show precisely how the disinformation process works and how we move from an open society to a closed society. You will see from the chart exactly where we are in the scheme of things in the disinformation process.

The end result is a destruction of private property and personal freedom. At that point, we will move into a closed society with the economic and political elite of the new world order running the show.

CHART 1: THE DISINFORMATION PROCESS

Demoralization (15-20 years)

AREAS	METHODS	RESULTS
Ideas		
1. Religion	Politicize, commercialize, entertainment	Death wish
2. Education	Permissiveness, relativity	Ignorance
3. Media	Monopolize, manipulate, discredit, non-issues	Uninformed media
4. Culture	False heroes and role models	Addictive fads, "mass"
Structure		
1. Law and order	Legislative, not moral	Mistrust "justice"
2. Social religion	Rights vs. obligations	Less individual responsibility
3. Security	Intelligence, police military	Defenselessness
4. Internal Politics	Party, antagonisms	Disunity
5. Foreign	Salt...friends	Isolation
Life		
1. Family, society	Break up	No loyalty (state)
2. Health	Sports, Medicare, junk food	Enfeebled masses
3. Race	Lower the uppers, Bible? Genetics vs. environment	Hatred, division
4. Population	De-land, urbanize	Alienation
5. Labor	Unions vs. society	Victimization

Destabilization (2 to 5 Years)

1. Power struggle	Populism, unresponsible	Big brother
2. Economy	Destruction of bargaining process	Yield to big brother
3. Society fiber, law	Grass roots participation	Mobocracy
4. Foreign	Isolation, multi-nations, and central committee,	Prestige, belligerence, encirclement

Crisis (2 to 6 months)

Normalization

Note: This chart prepared by Tomas Schuman, who defected to the United States after having served as a KGB disinformation agent.

CHART 2: THE MOVEMENT FROM AN OPEN
SOCIETY TO A CLOSED SOCIETY

Open Society

Egalitarianism

Expectations Up

Aspirations vs. Reality

Discontent

Productivity Down

Inflation and Unemployment=Recession

Social Unrest

Instability

Radicalism

Power Struggle

Replacement

Civil War, Revolution, and Invasion

Closed Society

CHAPTER 7

MYSTERIES OF COMMERCIAL BABYLON

s I have stated many times throughout this book, the new world order is nothing new and it is not going to be orderly. It is a code word for one-world socialism. I believe the new world order will come about in three phases, with phase one being the new economic order. But, once again, it's not new. It is simply old world economics, or commercial Babylon, dressed up in modern garb.

If you were to ask the average person what type of economic system we have, they would probably answer capitalism. That answer would be partially true. If you asked them what type of system is the opposite of our system, they would probably say communism, which also would be partially true. But we are not in a struggle between communism and capitalism, and we never have been.

Now, you may be thinking that I have really gone off my rocker. But before you put the book down, hear me out. The only economic system that exists in a modern world is a capitalistic system. Capital is nothing but the means of production. Therefore we must distinguish between consumer goods and capital goods.

Consumer goods are the clothes we wear, the food we eat, the roofs over our heads — in other words, something that satisfies a human need. On the other hand, capital goods are the means of production of consumer goods. Capital goods are the manufacturing plants, the trucks on the highways, the airplanes, the trains, the farm equipment in the fields — something that is a means of production.

I believe you will now agree with me that there is capital in the former Soviet Union. There are trains, planes, tractors, trucks on the highways, manufacturing plants — they are capital goods. Therefore, the former Soviet Union was a capitalist country.

Where, then, is the struggle? The struggle is between monopolistic capitalism and competitive capitalism as you see in chart 3 on the following page.

The characteristic of monopolistic capitalism is that capital is held privately or by the state, controlled by you or by the state; a further characteristic of that system is that prices are high, quality is poor, and there is generally no private property for the masses. Conversely, in a competitive capitalistic system, we have capital held privately, controlled privately; a further characteristic is that prices are low, the quality is high, and we produce so much that we have to hire people to go and sell the products.

CHART 3: ECONOMIC SYSTEMS

<u>Monopolistic Capitalism</u>
Capital held privately or by State.
Controlled by a few or by the State.
Prices – high; Quality – poor, No private property.

<u>Competitive Capitalism</u>
Capital held privately; Controlled privately.
Prices – low; Quality – high, Private property for all.

Under this system of competitive capitalism, we have private property for everyone who wants to work for it. Suppose this issue were posed to us on our ballots each year with the question, "Which do you choose — monopolistic capitalism with all of its characteristics, or competitive capitalism with all of its characteristics?" What do you suppose the outcome would be? Frankly, I think it would be no contest because everyone has a desire for low prices, high quality and the opportunity to own private property. Unfortunately, we do not get to vote on this question. So what determines whether we have a monopolistic or competitive capitalism system? That is determined by nothing more or nothing less than political systems. It is determined by politics. If you will note on chart 4, it is a true spectrum of political systems.

On the far left, you have total government; on the far right, you have anarchy or no one in control. In the center you have limited government. For all practical purposes, a monarchy or dictatorship does not exist in the world today.

CHART 4: POLITICAL SYSTEMS

System	Who Rules
Monarchy/Dictatorship	Rule by One
Oligarchy	Rule by Elite
Democracy	Rule by Majority
Republic	Rule by Law
Anarchy	Rule by None

Now many people thought that Saddam Hussein was a dictator in Iraq. But notice that in everything that Saddam Hussein does or considers, there is always a ruling military council around him, which means that it is an oligarchy (rule by the elite). The oligarchs rule in Iraq. The oligarchs rule in Russia. They are called the politburo.

At the far right is anarchy (no one is in control). It is a vacuum, and a vacuum will not last very long. It is natural that something will be sucked into a vacuum, and generally in a vacuum of anarchy the person swept into power will be the one that has the most and the biggest guns.

That leaves in the center limited government, democracy and republic.

If you ask the average third grader in our public schools today what type of political system we have in America, he or she would probably smile and say, "We live in the world's greatest democracy." Let me tell you emphatically that history shows that our founding fathers did not give us a democracy; they gave us a republic.

What's the difference? Let's assume that we are all attending a meeting of our democracy and I happen to be presiding over that meeting. Someone makes a motion and says, "Mr.

Chairman, I move that we take the property of all of those who are not here today, and I further move that we divide their property among ourselves." There is a second to the motion. We debate the issue; we take a vote and the motion passes. I appoint a policeman from our midst to bring in the absentees' property and divide it among ourselves.

By now you might be saying to yourself, "I wouldn't be a part of that. That's wrong!" Friend, that's what we're doing every day in Washington. We are passing laws that are taking from those who are productive and, under the force of law, we are giving their property to beneficiaries of the politicians' choice.

So why did our founding fathers not give us a democracy? Remember what Alfred Fraser Tyler said:

> A democracy can last as long and until a majority of the people discover they can vote themselves largesse (large gifts) out of the public treasury. They will continue to elect the politicians promising the most, with the end result being a fall of the democracy due to economic ruin and chaos.[1]

History shows us that our founding fathers gave us a republic, which is a rule by law. The law was to protect the individual. The republic was simply a collective force of individuals to protect the individual's right to life, liberty and property.

Our founding fathers gave us a republic because they knew very well that a democracy was simply a temporary and transitional form of government on the way to totalitarian government. Those founding fathers were freedom-loving people who wanted to avoid all forms of state monopoly such as communism, nazism, fascism and even socialism.

What is the driving force behind our political and economic systems? It's simple — money.

Money Moves the World

It often has been said that money does move the world. Therefore if you are of the mind to control the economic and social behavior of the masses, it is desirable to control the money.

In 1913, out of ignorance and some documented deceit, Congress gave the Federal Reserve a monopoly on the creation of paper money. Since that time, this country has existed as a discretionary monetary economy. At the discretion of the policy makers (federal reserve bankers), interest rates are set by the arbitrary expansion or contraction of the paper money supply, thus determining the course of our economy.

Over the years, these money managers or money creators have used carefully planned disinformation campaigns to maintain their monopoly on money and their control of the economy by making the system appear complex and impossible for anyone outside their league to understand. They have successfully purveyed the idea that we just can't do without them. Since their major tool of control is the control of money, they must keep the masses focused on the psychological money they control.

People with a "herd" mentality get involved in various investment vehicles without the slightest understanding of the underlying system that determines the value of their investments. That system is the monetary system. What is going on today is nothing new, as we will see as we read in Amos 8:5:

> When will the new moon be gone, that we may sell corn? and the sabbath, that we may set forth wheat, making the ephah [bushel] small, and the shekel [dollar] great, and falsifying the balances by deceit?

What we learned from history is that we don't learn from history. Our current monetary system, based on dishonest weights and measures, has trapped many well-meaning people, because they wanted to believe the lie. Adolph Hitler theorized:

> Tell the big lie long enough and often enough, and pretty soon most every one will believe it.[2]

What Is Money?

What is money? Most people would answer, "It's what I have in my purse or wallet," "It's what I have in my bank account," "It's what I have in my brokerage account," or a combination thereof. The common definition that we find in the dictionary for money is as follows:

> Money (mun-e) n.pl. a) standard pieces of gold, silver, copper, nickel, etc., stamped by government authority and used as a medium of exchange and a measure of value. Coin or coins, also called hard money; b) any paper note issued by government or an authorized bank and used in the same way: bank notes, bills, also called paper money.[3]

You might ask the question, "What did we do before we had money?" The answer is barter.

Suppose that I am a grain farmer. Joe is a dairy farmer and Sam doesn't farm, but he has a processing plant. I get tired of eating grain all of the time. I'd like to have some milk and meat. Joe gets tired of eating meat and drinking milk, and Sam, who has the processing plant, would like to have something to eat.

What do we do? I send grain to Sam and Joe, swapping for meat, milk, and the services of the processing plant.

In other words, all of us in our little economic unit either produced goods, as Joe and I did, or provided a service, as Sam did with his processing plant. But as we became a more mobile society, it became difficult to pick up the grain and carry it everywhere. It was difficult for Joe to carry his cows and it was difficult for Sam to pick up and move the processing plant around the country.

So what happened was the evolution of money. We saw money take on required characteristics in order to be considered money.

Money had to be something that everyone would accept in trade for various goods and services and that could later be exchanged with someone else for goods and services which they needed. This key concept of a portable medium of exchange gave a tremendous boost to trading and other economic activities. In other words, money had become the medium, or the middle man, of all transactions, making trade and commerce more convenient.

We see throughout the history of early civilization that the increasing trade in commerce caused people to gravitate to gold and silver as the trading medium. We see in the early days of the Bible that gold and silver had great value. People had long desired the precious metals for jewelry and decoration. It was valuable because it took labor to prospect for it, it took labor to mine it, and it took labor to refine it.

As time passed, a substance called electrum came into existence. Electrum was simply a mixture of gold and silver molded into a crude ball or lump. These lumps of electrum were used as the medium of exchange because everyone knew from experience these lumps would not lose their value. It was widely recognized as money, and change could be made by shaving off pieces of electrum until the proper weight for payment had been achieved.

After electrum in its crude form was being used, we saw the advent of coinage around 650 B.C. People still liked electrum, but coins were far better. Coins were pre-weighted and had different sizes and denominations. It was not necessary to shave off the pieces to make change.

With the advent of coinage, man's sinful nature rose up again. Kings and governments discovered a great secret. They could give themselves a monopoly of the mint by simply decreeing that only coins authorized by the king could be used. The king also put his image on the coins. He also had the opportunity to debase the coins and thereby steal from the people.

He did that by periodically calling in all the coins of the realm. He would then melt them, add a small amount of cheap base metal to the gold or silver and then re-mint them. Because he had added the base metal, he had more coins than before. They still were accepted at face value by the people when the king first spent them, because they didn't know any better.

This had become a "back-door" tax on the people. How?

It's simple. The one who gets the new money first or who knows about the new money first profits at the expense of the one who gets it last or knows about it last, because the king got to spend the money first. Many times he would create more coins to finance the war activities he was carrying on.

The most insidious thing about this back-door tax is the fact that the people didn't even know they were being taxed. That is fraud. Even back in the prophet Amos' day we read that they made "the ephah small, and the shekel great...falsifying the scales by deceit" (Amos 8:5).

As early civilization advanced and more trade and commerce took place, the coins became cumbersome and heavy to carry around. Someone discovered banking, and the people simply carried their coins to a depository and received a depository receipt showing how many coins were on deposit.

It became evident that it was far easier to transport the depository receipts than the actual coins; since the bankers would redeem the depository receipts and return the coins to whoever presented the receipt, it became common practice to trade the receipts rather than the actual coins. Thus, paper money came into existence.

The king then discovered he could do exactly the same thing with paper money that he had done with gold and that the bankers had done with the depository receipts. He printed pieces of paper that represented the quantity of gold or silver that he had in the royal treasury. Then by decree he made it illegal to use anything except his paper money (legal tender laws).

Over time the king gradually severed the relationship between the quantity of paper and quantity of gold or silver in the royal treasury until the paper was based on nothing but the good faith and credit of the king. After all, the legal tender laws declared that you had to use the king's money.

As more and more money was created, it became more plentiful. And as it became more plentiful, it had a diminished value. This is what we know today as inflation.

If we go to the dictionary for the definition of inflation, we read as follows:

> Inflation (infla-shun), noun: an inflating or being inflated; an increase in the amount of money and credit in relation to the supply of goods and services.[4]

Inflation is something like this: If I serve you a cup of black coffee and then start pouring clear hot water in your coffee to dilute it, and if your objective in drinking the coffee is the caffeine it contains, then you're going to have to drink a lot more coffee to get the same amount of caffeine. The same thing happens with our money. As we have more money printed and put into circulation, the result is a fall in its value and a rise in prices.

You may be asking by now, "What should money be then?" Money should be something that has all ten of the following characteristics. If it does, it will function as it should.

1. It should be a store of value. Your money should be worth, in terms of purchasing power, what it is worth today, next year, or even in ten years.
2. It should be easily recognizable as money. We can't expect someone to accept it as payment if they don't know what it is.

3. It should be universally acceptable. If people do not desire it, it has no value in trade.

4. It should be easily divisible. This is a must in order to make change.

5. It should have intrinsic value. It should be desirable in, and of, itself.

6. It should be impossible to counterfeit. If it cannot be counterfeited, it cannot be created out of nothing. If it cannot be created out of nothing, there can be no inflation and a resulting depreciation in its value.

7. It should be durable. If it is not durable and deteriorates or is easily destroyed, its value will not last over time.

8. It should have high value in small quantities. A concentration of value or wealth makes it more convenient to transport.

9. It must be easy to handle. It must be in a size and form easy to store, transport and exchange.

10. Its supply must remain scarce.

When we compare most of the paper currencies, including the U.S. Federal Reserve note dollar to this list, it has only three of the ten characteristics. Real money must have all ten. However, we must remember that people — not governments, central banks or even nation states — have always determined what money is and what money is not. They have always voted in the market place with their feet.

In all of recorded history, including the Holy Bible, we have seen that the currency of choice and the money of the Bible is gold and silver. We read in 1 Kings 10:2 that when the

Queen of Sheba came to visit King Solomon, she came bearing gold and precious stones (I cannot find anywhere in that text that she came bearing her CDs and municipal bond portfolios). This was the money of the day and it has remained so for thousands of years, to this very day.

In biblical times and continuing to this very day, there always has been that sin nature of man and his fatal tendency to live and consume off the labor of others. The Babylonian monetary system is alive and well in the world today in the form of dishonest weights and measures. Our monetary system today is doing the very same thing that is mentioned in Amos 8:5. We are making the ephah (or bushel or whatever we're buying) smaller and the shekel (or dollar as we know it today) larger by inflating it so that it buys less goods, and we cheat with dishonest scales.

This is an abomination to almighty God. This is a system, a commercial Babylonian system, that He already has judged; it is a system that we as believers must come out of. It's really simple. When you don't use the king's (the government's) money, the king (the government) can't rip you off.

You don't need legal tender laws to tell people what money they should use. You only need legal tender laws when the money that is being used is not what the market place desires but is being forced upon the people by the edict of the king or the decree of the government.

If one is to survive this coming economic disorder, one must learn what money is and what money is not. When people understand, there will be a mad rush to dump the counterfeit and grab the real thing.

Don't you think it's strange that the Federal Reserve (private bank) who was given by the king (Congress and the president) in 1913 a monopoly on the creation of paper money has more than 50 percent of its assets in gold?

We must remember that the gold at the Federal Reserve is not for our benefit. Nowhere on the the Federal Reserve's notes that we carry around in our wallets does it say that they are redeemable for part of the gold. The bills we accept as money are simply IOUs of the Federal Reserve.

Try to find on the face of any Federal Reserve note what it owes you; you will find that it says it owes you nothing. Therefore, you are carrying around a pocket full of "IOU nothings."

I challenge you now to pull out any bill in your wallet and examine it carefully. If you have a one dollar bill and you ask the average person on the street to identify this bill for you, they will, in most instances, say it is a dollar. I must tell you that it is not a dollar.

The word dollar comes from the Greek word *thaler* which means "unit of measurement." Congress defined a dollar as so many grains of gold.

Suppose you saw me pick up a two-pound bag of coffee at the local supermarket. You were behind me in the checkout line as I said to the clerk, "Just pour out the coffee and give me the two pounds." What would you think? I know what you would think. You would think, "Wow, he's really lost it!" But that's exactly what you've done with your dollar.

We've all said together, "Just forget the gold; give me the dollar." This is precisely how the economic and political elite of this world have been able to accomplish the biggest Robin Hood theft of all times. They have simply taken from the ignorant and given it to themselves, the well informed.

You must be asking yourself right now, "What kind of system would allow something like this to go on?" That's easy — the one we've got. But wait. As Paul Harvey says, you need to hear "the rest of the story."

Chapter 8

PARTNERS IN CRIME

It has been said, "When elephants stampede, the grass gets trampled." I know you're thinking, "Wait a minute. What does that have to do with the subject matter at hand?" A lot. Let's use an example of two rogue elephants joining together to ravage the landscape. These two rogue elephants are the elephant of commercial Babylon joining with the elephant of political Babylon and going on the biggest crime spree in thousands of years.

It always has been the nature of kings and rulers to bestow gifts and favors upon their subjects to incur their favor. It also has been their habit to devise ways to control their subjects by giving them gifts they had acquired or stolen from other subjects when their own money ran out.

Government, by nature, does not produce anything. It can only take from those who are productive and give it to the beneficiaries of the politicians' choice. The framers of our Constitution never intended that government provide for us; they intended that government merely protect us. However, over the years Congress, the president and the courts have strayed from that intent and have used legalized plunder (taking from some Americans by force of law and giving their property to others of the politicians' choice) to serve the politicians' self-interest rather than the public interest.

If we carefully examine many of the recent elections, we will find that most winners promise to "take from Peter and give to Paul," and in return receive Paul's support. Surprisingly, in many cases these same politicians received Peter's support too, because Peter didn't know he was being robbed.

Now, what does all of this mean to you and me? It means that many of our politicians have discovered the art of political entrepreneurship. They have conducted nationwide or district polls to discern the so-called desires of their constituents. They see which way the crowd is going, then suddenly appear before the crowd saying, "Hey, I'm your new leader!" They tell the people they supposedly are leading that they are going to give them what they want — something for nothing.

In the boldest government initiative since the advent of the social security system, President Bill Clinton launched a plan for national health care that is loaded with massive taxes and spending. It also creates a gigantic government bureaucracy designed to make everyone more dependent upon government. This plan has nothing to do with health care. This plan has to do with control.

It is the goal of the new world order to control the economic and social behavior of everyone. Right here in the United States there is being established from among the party faithful a new and expanded ruling class to manage those who are not part of their enlightened ilk.

The term "party faithful" does not describe Democrats exclusively, but also describes Republicans who have sold out to the "government party" and are faithful to its causes. Many times these so-called moderate Republicans will endorse key parts of the socialist plan in order to be politically correct, but then will offer as an alternative a cheaper brand of socialism.

Such is the case in the health care debate, where Republican leadership of both the House and Senate has embraced (despite their rhetoric to the contrary) two of the key tenets of Clinton's socialist plan: universal coverage and government-mandated coverage. These Democrats and Republicans alike are promoting socialism. One only has to go to *Webster's New World Dictionary* to read the following definition of socialism:

> Socialism, noun: Any of various theories or systems of the ownership and operation of the means of production and distribution by society or the community rather than private individuals with all members of society or the community sharing in the work and the products; a political movement for establishing such a system, the doctrines, methods, etc., of the socialist parties; the stage of society in Marxist doctrine coming between the capitalist stage and the communist stage in which private ownership of the means of production and distribution has been eliminated.[1]

This proposal by President Clinton is not about health care at all; he and his socialist allies are using a "hot button issue" to promote a scheme that will ultimately control the economic and social behavior of everyone. Many may say, "This sounds far fetched," or "Show me some proof." One has only to look to the book *Tragedy and Hope* written by Dr. Carroll Quigley, Bill Clinton's mentor and professor at Georgetown University, to find these words:

> The individual's freedom and choice will be controlled within very narrow alternatives by the fact that he will be numbered from birth...and followed as a number through his educational training, his required military or other service, his tax contributions, his health and medication requirements, and his final retirement and death benefits.[2]

General Douglas MacArthur wrote:

> Socialism, once a reality, destroys the moral fiber which is the creation of freedom. It breeds every device which produces totalitarian rule.[3]

We have made stealing under the pretense of law a way of life. We have further glorified a legal system that authorizes it; and we have, by default, adopted a moral code that gives it credibility.

Government, as envisioned by our founding fathers, was not supposed to become our national nanny. Our founding fathers staked the whole future of American civilization upon the capacity of each and every one of us to govern and support ourselves according to the Ten Commandments of God.

We are now getting to the heart of the matter. This war of world views has intensified on the plains with these two rogue elephant herds (commercial Babylon and political Babylon) that have joined together.

Ever since his fall in the Garden of Eden man has been in a state of rebellion; many times he has swallowed the bait on the pagan hook, "You shall be as gods." This was the deception that men fell prey to when, on the plains of Shinar thousands of years ago, they attempted to build the Tower of Babel as a monument to man's power and importance. What we see today is man's attempt to replace God with man's government as controller and provider of everything. This is simply a resurrecting of the old Babylonian spirit.

On September 22, 1993, U.S. President Bill Clinton stood before a joint session of Congress, flashed a health security card, and proclaimed:

> We must make this our urgent priority. Give every American health care security; health care that can never be taken away; heath care that is always there.

In the process Clinton tossed out the mythical number of 37 million American who allegedly have no health insurance. A study by the National Center for Policy Analysis cites data from the U.S. Public Health Service,

> Only 1.8 million, or less than 1 percent of the population, cannot obtain health insurance because of health reasons (uninsurable).[4]

It is estimated that another 2 percent cannot afford health

insurance because they are part of the 6 percent unemployed in the country. Many by choice do not have health insurance, as they have found better ways to spend their money. Should we play national nanny to all of these people? Yes, if you believe in socialism. No, if you believe in freedom and liberty.

Bill Clinton's programs in this country constitute only one part of the worldwide plan to bring us rapidly into a new world order.

The nagging question remains, "How will we pay for all of these glorious benefits that our socialist politicians want to shower on us?" The answer to that is fairly simple. The government can only obtain money to spend from one of, or a combination of, three sources. It either has to tax the money, borrow the money or print the money.

Let's Tax It

There are those who argue that we must raise taxes to balance the budget. Those who argue this are genuinely, ideologically committed to totalitarian government, where government owns and controls everything — including the individual. Taxing the full expenditure would mean that we would have less take-home pay to spend as we desire and would require us to send increased amounts of our hard-earned money to Washington for politicians to bestow upon the beneficiaries of their choice. I estimate that to balance the budget by increasing taxes would mean the average American would have approximately 40 percent less take-home pay than they have today.

What would this do to our economy? It would collapse the economy. I don't care how much money you make. If you take 40 percent out of any household budget, you will have to make critical choices. Do you cut out housing, food, health care, clothing, transportation, education, communication or recreation? What do you cut out? You will have to cut something if you have to live on 40 percent less take-home pay than you currently have.

This not only would collapse the private sector of our economy, it would even worsen the deficit. Since this is obviously not a solution, what other options do we have to fund government spending?

Borrow It

Borrowing the money is what we have been doing for many years; this is why our national debt is almost $5 trillion. Let's say the government spends $1.5 trillion for all of its programs and takes in revenues of $1 trillion dollars. The government has spent more money than it took in. How do you and I pay our bills if we spend more than we take in? We either don't, or we borrow the money.

Suppose you and I line up at the loan window of our local bank to borrow money to buy a new home, a new car, expand our plant facility or to plant a crop. The federal government comes to fund the deficit. Who is going to get the money and how much are we going to pay for what is left?

The only amounts available for the government or anyone to borrow are what someone else has saved. The net national savings of the United States has been running only a little over $500 billion per year. This means the federal government's borrowing needs would soak up almost all of the available funds. In an open market this would cause interest rates to approach 100 percent.

What would this do to our economy? Again, it would collapse the private sector of our nation and worsen the deficit. Obviously this is not totally the answer either. So what is left?

Print It

Here is where the partnership between the money manipulators and their political enforcers (i.e., bankers and government leaders) really gets tight.

Before we address the area of printing, we must point out that Mr. Greenspan and the boys at the Federal Reserve have attempted to avoid monetizing or "printing" the deficit by various means. Foremost of these means was to keep real interest rates (market rate minus inflation) artificially high to attract foreign investors to buy the government's debt and thus delay the inevitable inflation until the appointed time. We must remember that this investment by foreigners is nothing but a claim check on our goods and services. The major consequence of such a policy has been the massive trade deficit, which itself must be financed.

We have now just about tapped out this source of financing as foreigners are becoming increasingly skeptical of our fiscal policies. Thus, the dollar will remain under intense pressure against foreign currencies.

I heard a former West German chancellor remark recently, "The U.S. will have to print money just to pay interest on its debt." Under the Federal Reserve Act of 1913 we gave the Federal Reserve a monopoly on the creation of paper money. In its self-appointed role of managing the nation's money supply and economy, the Federal Reserve has no option but to print. Taxation of the full expenditure would collapse the economy. Borrowing the full expenditure would be equally devastating, resulting in unbearably high interest rates.

We obviously have not learned a lesson from our neighbors to the south. Argentina and Brazil proved that government cannot continually spend beyond their means without facing the economic consequences. It defies logic to think that the United States can be the first to successfully avoid catastrophe when it continues to rely on the resources of other countries to finance its excesses.

Noted market analysist R.E. McMaster in *The Reaper* points out that since 1969 the Arab currencies, the Cuban peso, the Malaysian ringgit and even the Iranian rial all have appreciated against the dollar.[5]

Teruo Yonemura, an economist and executive director of Japan's International Businessmen's Club, told me that Japan did not want dollars. "We have quite enough dollars," he said. When I asked whether the G-7 industrialized nations would likely support the dollar or not, he replied, "Nations have a tendency to support their own interests."

That is precisely why the oil shock will exacerbate the decline of the dollar. Oil is priced worldwide in dollars; the oil shock, as oil prices continue to go up, is cushioned in Japan, England or Germany when the dollar declines.

Let's say the dollar declines by 20 percent against a foreign currency and oil is selling for $30 per barrel. That equates in real terms to $24 per barrel of oil instead of $30 per barrel of oil for the foreigners. Do you really think they will support the dollar? They will only give lip service to supporting the dollar in order to save their own economy.

You have to understand that we do not have a revenue problem; we have a spending problem. The only sound answer to the economy would be to balance the budget by cutting spending. But is this going to happen? Unfortunately not. It hasn't happened yet, and as of May 31, 1994, the summary of public debt outstanding was in excess of $4.5 trillion.[6]

The balancing of the budget will not happen because politicians, like drug addicts, will have to have another "fix" in order to fulfill their promises to the beneficiaries of their choice. The end result will be economic ruin and chaos, brought on by deliberate policy actions to increase the nation's money supply.

As we've mentioned before, *Webster* defines inflation as, "an increase in the amount of money in circulation, resulting in a fall in its value and a rise in prices."[7]

Politicians will opt for inflation as the least noticed way to fund their political promises. Americans believe that economic chaos can't happen as we pursue this insane national policy of unchecked spending; yet, history shows that we are well along the road to national suicide.

What can we do about it? Later on, I'll give you some concrete recommendations of how to protect yourself and your family from this economic disorder, which is well advanced and heading toward us like a herd of stampeding elephants.

What we must do is continue to raise our level of understanding of where the two rogue elephants and their bands of followers are headed and make sure that our family and our assets are well out of their path. Remember, when elephants stampede, the grass — and everything else in their paths — gets trampled.

But wait! As they say on television, "There's more!"

Chapter 9

THE HEART OF POWER

The Federal Reserve System

On September 30, 1941, a very sharp exchange took place between Congressman Wright Patman, long an adversary of the Federal Reserve, and Marriner Eccles, then chairman of the Federal Reserve Board. The setting was a hearing before the House Banking and Currency Committee. The exchange went as follows:

Patman: Mr. Eccles, how did you get the money to buy those $2 billion of government securities?
Eccles: We created it.
Patman: Out of what?

Eccles: Out of the right to issue credit money.[1]

This is the same system that Sir Josiah Stamp, former president of the Bank of England in the 1920s and heralded as the second richest man in Britain, referred to when he said:

> Banking was conceived in iniquity and was born in sin. The bankers own the earth; take it away from them but leave them the power to create deposits, and with a flick of a pen they will create enough deposits to buy it back again. However, take it away from them and all the great fortunes like mine will disappear, and they ought to disappear, for this would be a happier and better world to live in. But if you wish to remain the slaves of bankers and pay the cost of your own slavery, let them continue to create deposits.[2]

One of the great patriarchs of the church, Martin Luther, was equally as strong in condemning such a system even connected to religion. He attacked the Catholic church for its involvment in banking and politics, particularly the office of the papacy which had become deeply involved in the political life of Western Europe. In describing the reformation, *The New Encylopedia Brittannica* says, "The resulting intrigues and political manipulations, combined with the church's increasing power and wealth, contributed to the bankrupting of the church as a spiritual force."[3]

It was that great president from Tennessee, Andrew Jackson, better known as Old Hickory, who said in his message in July of 1832 when vetoing the National Banking Act, a bill for renewal of the bank charter for a national, central bank:

It is to be regretted that the rich and powerful too often bend the ax of government to their selfish purposes. Distinctions in society will also exist under every just government. Equality of talents, of education, or of wealth cannot be produced by human institutions. In the full enjoyment of the gifts of heaven and the fruits of superior industry, economy, and virtue, every man is equally entitled to protection by the law. But when the laws undertake to add to these natural and just advantages, artificial distinctions to grant titles, gratuities and exclusive privileges; to make the rich richer and the potent more powerful, the humble members of society, the farmers, mechanics and laborers who have neither the time nor the means of securing like favors to themselves, have a right to complain of the injustice of the government.[4]

Andrew Jackson saw the bank's charter expire in 1836 and he even survived an assassination attempt, but the bankers were not about to give up their fight for central banking and a monopoly of the mint. Many banking interest groups in the United States and Europe were busy at work and even involved in the promotion of our Civil War.

After years of planning and fighting many battles, the International Banking establishment triumphed in 1913. This had been a carefully crafted plan, as many of the people involved in designing the Federal Reserve Act had met in secret at Jekyll Island, Georgia, on November 22, 1910. Those in attendance included key members of the National Monetary Commission and representatives of the largest banking interests in the country.

Robert W. Lee, writing in *Conservative Digest,* November 1985, quoted B.C. Forbes (who later founded *Forbes Magazine*) as he described the situation in *Current Opinion* for December, 1960:

> Picture a party of the nation's greatest bankers stealing out of New York on a private railroad car under cover of darkness, stealthily hieing hundreds of miles south, embarking on a mysterious launch, sneaking onto an island deserted by all but a few servants, living there a full week under such rigid secrecy that the names of not one of them was once mentioned lest the servants learn the identity and disclose to the world this strangest, most secret expedition in the history of American finance. I am not romancing; I am giving to the world for the first time the real story of how the famous Aldrich Currency Report, the foundation of our new currency system, was written. The utmost secrecy was enjoined upon all. The public must not glean a hint of what was to be done. Senator Aldrich notified each one to go quietly into a private car, which the railroad had received orders to draw up on an unfrequented platform.

Robert Lee goes on to say that the purpose of this strange gathering was to formulate plans for a central bank, to be privately owned, which would issue currency and control the nation's credit. It was to be called a regional reserve system, rather than a central bank to camouflage the dominant role to be played by the New York Reserve Bank.[5]

After years of planning and fighting many battles, the international banking establishment triumphed on December 23, 1913, with the passage of the Federal Reserve Act of 1913.

The average individual who lacked understanding must have been wondering what the fight was all about. Anything with the name of bank was considered a place where one could conveniently deposit or borrow money and write checks for the payment for goods and services.

After all, the stated goals of the Federal Reserve were very noble. These stated goals included maintaining stable economic growth, a low level of unemployment, stability in the purchasing power of the dollar, and maintaining a satisfactory balance of payments when transacting business with other countries.

Give 'em an "F"

That's right — an "F" for failure in achieving their stated goals (assuming it was their real intent in the first place). All one has to do is examine the peaks and valleys, booms and busts, since 1913 and conclude it's been anything but stable. Ask those who have ever been unemployed over the years; they'll tell you unemployment has, at times, been very high. Let's examine the dollar's purchasing power. Since 1940, the value of the dollar in 1940 dollars has dropped to less than $.03. If that's stability, then I would hate to see instability. In the area of balance of payments, we're continuing to experience the largest deficits in our balance of payments than ever recorded in our country's history. This can be attributed to a deliberate policy by the Federal Reserve system.

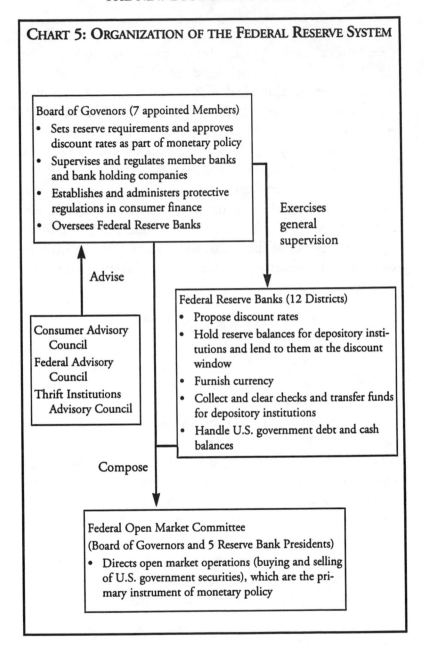

CHART 5: ORGANIZATION OF THE FEDERAL RESERVE SYSTEM

Board of Govenors (7 appointed Members)
- Sets reserve requirements and approves discount rates as part of monetary policy
- Supervises and regulates member banks and bank holding companies
- Establishes and administers protective regulations in consumer finance
- Oversees Federal Reserve Banks

Exercises general supervision

Advise

Consumer Advisory Council
Federal Advisory Council
Thrift Institutions Advisory Council

Federal Reserve Banks (12 Districts)
- Propose discount rates
- Hold reserve balances for depository institutions and lend to them at the discount window
- Furnish currency
- Collect and clear checks and transfer funds for depository institutions
- Handle U.S. government debt and cash balances

Compose

Federal Open Market Committee
(Board of Governors and 5 Reserve Bank Presidents)
- Directs open market operations (buying and selling of U.S. government securities), which are the primary instrument of monetary policy

It's Really an "A"

They deserve an "F" for failing their stated objectives, but they deserve an "A" for achieving their real goals of wealth transfer and being successful in pulling the wool over the eyes of a majority of Americans.

A Benign Looking Structure

The organization of the Federal Reserve system is composed of several parts. Its principal components are the board of governors of the Federal Reserve system, the federal open market committee (FOMC), the Federal Reserve banks and its branches, and member banks. The system also makes use of advisory and working committees to help handle its expansive and supposedly complex functions. Examples of those committees are the Federal Advisory Council, the Consumer Advisory Council and the Thrift Institutions Advisory Council (See Chart 5 on page 126).

The Board of Governors of the Federal Reserve System

The organization of the Federal Reserve system may be viewed as a pyramid. At the top is the Board of Governors, which is most commonly addressed as the Federal Reserve Board. The Board consists of seven members appointed by the president of the United States and confirmed by the Senate for a period of fourteen years each. The terms are staggered so that one expires every two years in even numbered years; members may not be re-appointed after serving a full term.

The chairman and the vice chairman of the Board are selected by the president of the United States and also are confirmed by the Senate.

It is important to note that even though its members are appointed by the president and confirmed by the Senate, the decisions of the Federal Reserve do not have to be approved by them. The system pays for its operating expenses out of assessments imposed on the Federal Reserve banks. With income obtained from open market operations they create money and use it to buy government securities on which they, in turn, receive interest. Interest on these securities is paid by you the taxpayer.

Since the system is not funded with government monies, it is often characterized as a central bank independent within government. However, this independence is subdued by the fact that Congress has the power to abolish the system if it wants to. Yet Congress lacks the courage.

In addition to supervising the operation of the twelve Federal Reserve banks, the Board regulates the supply of money and credit within the economy by authorizing the purchase or sale of government securities by the Federal Reserve banks, by setting the percentage of deposits that member banks are obliged to maintain as required reserves, and by altering the discount rate (interest rate) that member banks are required to pay when they borrow from Reserve banks. The Board also sets the margin (down payment) required on all credit purchases of stock securities by the public.

The Board also regulates and supervises the activities of member banks, such as international banking operations in the United States, foreign activities of U.S. banks, bank holding companies and bank mergers.

The Board is required to submit to Congress an annual report. Twice a year it must report on the state of the economy and target growth rates for money and credit. That is generally when you see the chairman of the Federal Reserve Board testifying before the respective Senate and House Banking Committees.

A Look Inside Their Tool Box

In order to implement the nation's monetary policy, the Federal Reserve system uses powerful and important tools which allow it to modify or reverse the course of the U.S. economy. The most important of these instruments are federal open market operations, discount rate, reserve requirements, margin requirements, and moral suasion (or reassuring babble).

The first three are general policy instruments, designed to affect the nation's money supply and credit availability. Margin requirements focus specifically on the stock market. Moral suasion, or reassuring babble, is a more subtle tool that relies on public opinion and appeals to bankers by public officials to expand or restrict credit without specifically requesting compliance.

Federal Open Market Operations

The Federal Reserve has the power to increase or decrease the money available to the American economy in many ways. One way is through open market operations. This tool is implemented by the Federal Open Market Committee (FOMC) through the New York Federal Reserve Bank. These operations consist of the purchase or sale of U.S. government securities by the Federal Reserve on the open market. "Open market" means that the Federal Reserve purchases the securities in the secondary, or resale, market and not directly from the issuer of the security.

When the Federal Reserve buys government securities in the open market from member banks or the general public, it pays for them by increasing the balances of the accounts member banks maintain at the Federal Reserve, or in the case of individuals, by giving them a check drawn on itself (the Federal Reserve). In both cases the effect is an increase in the amount of money in circulation.

When the Federal Reserve sells government securities to member banks or to the general public, the buyers pay by transferring money from their accounts maintained at the Federal Reserve to the Federal Reserve itself; individuals pay by drawing checks on their accounts at commercial banks, which reduces their deposit balances. In each case the amount of money in circulation decreases.

Federal open market operations use the single most important monetary instrument available to the Federal Reserve. This tool allows the Federal Reserve to exert direct control on the amount of money in circulation and therefore influence the cost and availability of credit.

Unlike other tools which are very blunt, this is a more flexible and subtle tool, almost like a surgeon's scalpel, which allows the Federal Reserve the opportunity of performing market intervention on a daily basis. The immediate impact of these interventions is hard to evaluate, even by experienced Federal Reserve watchers.

Discount Rate

The discount rate is the interest rate the Federal Reserve charges its member banks when they temporarily borrow from the system. For this reason, the Federal Reserve is sometimes referred to as the banker's bank.

This rate is called a discount rate because the interest due on the loans is discounted at the time the loan is made rather than paid at the time when the loan becomes due. The banks can borrow either by giving their own promissory notes or by re-discounting loans previously made to their customers. Unlike open market operations, which are initiated by the Federal Reserve, discounting is initiated by the member banks.

In any case, the Federal Reserve has made it clear that discounting should be viewed only as a temporary means of replenishing depleted reserves that cannot be met through alternative sources, not as a permanent source of credit. This is the safety net for the banks in case of having a liquidity crisis or run on the bank.

Changes in the discount rate also are used to signal Federal Reserve intentions to the markets and counteract inflationary or recessionary forces in the economy. While an increase in the discount raises the cost of borrowing for member banks, a decrease has the opposite effect. These changes directly affect member banks' cost of borrowing and indirectly influence the direction of most other money market rates and credit conditions in the economy.

In order to make Federal Reserve intervention more effective and flexible, discount rates changes are often coordinated with their open market operations.

Reserve Requirements

The commercial banking system operates on what is called a fractional reserve basis. This means that these commercial banks are required by law to maintain a certain percentage of a customer's deposit as a legal, or required, reserve. These reserves may be kept in the form of vault cash (Federal Reserve notes) or deposits at a Federal Reserve bank.

This fractional reserve banking system operates on the banker's widely held belief that it is very unlikely that all bank depositors would demand all of their money deposits at any one time. They believe a money cushion or reserve (as paltry as it may be) is needed in order to meet normal withdrawals; they lend the rest and even create more for a profit. In this way, banks benefit from the interest rate spread that exists between the rate paid to you the depositor and the rate charged on loans.

These legal reserve requirements determine the amount of new money banks can create and make available to new customers; therefore they affect the size of the money supply and the economy as a whole. While an increase in legal requirements tends to be contractionary because it decreases the size of the money supply and credit availability, a decrease in legal reserve requirements tends to be expansionary because it increases them.

The ability to alter the legal reserve percentage of requirement is a very powerful monetary policy instrument. It is a blunt ax and inflexible tool; for this reason the Federal Reserve in the past has used it relatively sparingly.

In the event there should be a run on the banks, the Federal Reserve requested, lobbied for, and was successful in getting passed the Monetary Control Act of 1980. A provision of that Act allows the Federal Reserve to reduce reserve requirements to zero.

Margin Requirements

The Board of Governors of the Federal Reserve is empowered by the Securities Exchange Act of 1934 and its amendments to regulate the purchase of securities (stock) on margin (credit).

Margin is the minimum down payment that a borrower must make when purchasing stock on credit. In this case, the stock must be pledged as collateral.

An example might help clarify this concept. If the Board of Governors were to set a margin requirement of 80 percent and an investor intended to buy stock valued at $100,000 on credit, the cash advance would be $80,000. On the other side, if the margin were set at 30 percent, the investor would need to put down only $30,000 on the same purchase.

By simply altering the margin requirements the Federal Reserve can exert enormous direct and very blunt influence on stock market activities. While an increase in the margin requirements will tend to discourage stock market speculation, a decrease in those same requirements will have the exact opposite effect.

Excessive use of credit was one of the factors that led to people getting taken down in the stock market crash of 1929. Margin requirements have been altered on several occasions by the Federal Reserve, but at present they stand at 50 percent. If you wanted to buy stock on credit, that same $100,000 stock purchase would require you to advance $50,000 on the purchase.

Moral Suasion, or Reassuring Babble

As I previously stated, moral suasion is a more subtle monetary policy tool that relies on public opinion and appeals to bankers by public officials to expand or restrict credit without specifically requesting or demanding their compliance.

It is particularly in this respect that the independence of the Federal Reserve is questioned; on past occasions these jawboning techniques may well have influenced more decisions to produce the desired political results or prevent certain market actions or even head off runs on commercial banks.

A more accommodative monetary policy is highly desirable by the incumbent party in an election year because it would boost the economy to make things look rosier than perhaps they really are. The consequences of this policy would be highly inflationary in the long run. In fact, I have observed some cases where it appeared that the Federal Reserve had become "the committee to re-elect the president."

In reality, the use of these discretionary tools over the years has resulted in our economy being fragile. It is so fragile that the only glue holding this economy together is the reassuring babble that's coming out of the mouths of public officials and central bankers in this country and around the world.

When you analyze that statement, we have to conclude that this whole system is nothing but a confidence game; they are conning people every day and convincing them that the system is safe and they have nothing to worry about because the Federal Reserve is looking after their interests. In reality, the Federal Reserve has used the creation of psychological money as the muscle behind their bully pulpit.

Money

Most people think of money only as the amount in their bank account, in their wallet, or in their mutual fund; they never consider the properties that real money should possess as discussed in a previous chapter. Nor have they considered the prospects that one day their money may have little or no value.

The ultimate demise of the value of what most people now call money is totally in the care, custody and control of the Federal Reserve. Remember that the Federal Reserve, created in 1913 by an act of Congress, gave this private bank a monopoly on the creation of paper money in the form of Federal Reserve notes, commonly referred to as currency.

A note is nothing but an IOU. A close examination of these notes shows that they are in reality "I owe you nothings." The days are long gone when those notes existed that promised to pay you in gold or in silver coin of the United States. Our gold was confiscated at the stroke of a pen by President Franklin D. Roosevelt in 1933; President Lyndon B. Johnson took the silver out of your dimes, quarters and half dollars in 1965.

All this was necessary for the Federal Reserve to consolidate its power and expand its control over the economy. They can't print honest money, such as silver and gold. Therefore, they had to perpetuate the total usage of fiat money in order for the Federal Resreve to achieve its goal of total economic enslavement of this country.

They cannot afford to have any vestige of sound money in circulation; history shows that good money always drives out bad. There would be a tremendous demand for the good money unless they extinguished silver and gold from the landscape of American currency.

In order to keep the average person from discovering what is really happening, these bankers have over the years used lofty and arcane language to describe money. Again I refer you to the definition of money as "standard pieces of copper, nickel, silver, gold...paper notes, etc., stamped by government authority and used as a medium of exchange and a measure of value."

The Federal Reserve refers to money as M-1, M-2, M-3, L, etc. Don't let those fancy economic terms snow you, because they are really pretty simple.

M-1 (basic money supply) is simply cash and currency in circulation, plus demand deposits. It's everybody's pocket cash plus their checkbook money put together.

M-2 (broad base money supply) is M-1 plus savings. M-2 is nothing more than pocket cash, checkbook money, and savings account money put together. All of those components are nothing but IOUs in some form, from somebody or institution that in the end will never be redeemed, or they will be redeemed with more worthless IOUs.

Monetary Policy

Monetary policy is nothing but a fancy code word for the phrase, "It's how we fleece those dumb sheep." The Federal Reserve, as I have mentioned throughout this book, has a monopoly on the creation of paper money. Monetary policy, therefore, becomes discretionary at the discretion of the Federal Reserve because they decide how much new money and credit should be created or destroyed to achieve certain aims of the economic and political elite.

Inflation of the currency is a form of confiscation; that is why one must understand the system in order to avoid being fleeced by what is glorified in the term monetary policy. My friend economist Walter Williams has suggested, "The next time you are brought up on counterfeiting charges, just tell the judge that you were engaged in monetary policy."

Creation of a Monster

It has been said many times that men left to their own devices eventually will destroy themselves. The Federal Reserve's unbridled expansion of money and credit has created a debt monster of gigantic proportions that either has to be serviced or it will default.

Current domestic debt (federal, state, county, municipal, corporate, mortgage and consumer debt) exceeds $12.5 trillion and is growing at an ever-increasing rate of between $60 billion and $70 billion per month. This debt figure does not include all of the contingent liabilities of government or financial institution bailout costs, which are estimated at another $15 trillion to $20 trillion.

This debt also has to be serviced; it's not free. The bankers are charging interest. The servicing of this debt requires the Federal Reserve to always be in a posture of creating more money in order to stave off a collapse.

Let's look at a short, concise example. Let's say you borrow $10,000 at 10 percent interest. At the end of the year, the banker wants back $10,000, plus $1,000 for interest. However, the $1,000 for interest doesn't exist. The banker only created $10,000, but he wants back more than he loaned you. This is a flaw in our monetary system, and it is precisely why it will not work for very much longer.

Here's what happens: You pay your principal of $10,000,

which leaves you the interest debt of $1,000. Because there is no money with which you can pay it if the Federal Reserve does not increase the money supply of the economy, you will have to start your second year of borrowing $1,000 more in debt. Assume you borrow, for whatever purpose, another $10,000; you now owe $10,000 plus the prior interest of $1,000 — $11,000 at 10 percent interest. By the end of the second year, you owe $12,100 ($11,000 principal, plus $1,100 interest).

This is simply compound interest in full operation, but your banker will continue to loan you more money as long as you have unmortgaged collateral (home, farm, equipment, etc.) with which he can secure the loan.

This increased borrowing to pay interest has now become a part of your business; in order for you to continue you must pass this extra cost on to the consumer. If you are not in business this increased cost of borrowing will be passed on to your employer when you say to him, "I must have a raise in order to meet my increased expenses of paying interest to the banker."

All of this within itself is inflationary. The Federal Reserve anticipates this and therefore inflates the currency and provides the increased money supply in the form of new money and credit. This is nothing more than a system of bondage that keeps the borrower always in debt to the bankers because of a dishonest system of banking, money and credit. This is precisely why the Word of God tells us repeatedly, "The borrower is servant to the lender" (Prov. 22:7).

The biggest evil about interest (tithe to the world system) is that it cannot be paid; interest is always compounded. J.A. Thauberger has calculated and shown a very vivid example of the evils of compound interest in his booklet *Billions for the Bankers*. He says,

> Let me give an example of the difference between compound interest and simple interest. One dollar loaned out at the time of the birth of Christ at 3 percent compound interest would be a debt of $19,342,814,713,834,066,795,298,816. At 6 percent interest, it would be $2,075,564,540,495,770, 000,659,356,622,933,159,968,008,080,198,784. At simple interest, the interest would be $59 and $118, respectively."[6]

With this ever increasing and mounting debt burden caused by compounding interest, the banker is always in a position of calling your note and repossessing your collateral at his discretion, or he will continue to create money so that you are working for him and paying interest (tithe to the world system) if you are to play his game.

One of the slickest methods ever devised to transfer wealth was the fractional reserve banking system, whereby bankers create money out of nothing. They not only charge you interest, but they charge you interest on that which they created out of nothing. You see, bankers are not loaning you money; bankers are loaning you credit of the bank.

PFA Banking

"Pluck From Air"? That's right — pluck from air. That's how commercial banks create money. The Federal Reserve is the engine of inflation, but commercial banks are the transmission attached to the engine. The Federal Reserve, through the FOMC (Federal Open Market Committee), adds or renews banks' reserves from the money system. Local banks, through lending, multiply those reserves and increase the money locally.

As a former banker, I have literally created millions of dollars out of thin air with the stroke of my pen. It works like this:

One day I made a loan to a customer in the amount of $100,000, thereby increasing my assets in loans by $100,000. This customer was a good customer, and I deposited the $100,000 loan proceeds to my customer's checking account, thereby increasing my liabilities on the liabilities side of my bank ledger by $100,000. At the end of the day when I totaled my statement of condition, by the stroke of my pen I had increased the size of my bank by $100,000.

All I have to do legally is to keep 10 percent of the $100,000 I deposited to my customer's checking account, or $10,000, in reserve. I subtract this $10,000 from the $100,000 deposit, and I now loan my next customer $90,000 of their money and repeat the process.

The total amount that I can ultimately create is called a "multiplier." It is determined by a formula which is regulated by the reserve requirement set by the Federal Reserve.

If you were to have a 10 percent reserve requirement, a simple way to determine the multiplier is to divide 100 by your reserve requirement. In the case of 100 divided by 10 percent reserve, it equals 10, so your multiplier factor is 10. In other words, with a 10 percent reserve requirement, I can take $1,000,000 in new deposits and under fractional reserve banking can parlay that into a maximum of $10,000,000 in newly created money supply.

Again let me emphasize that under the Monetary Control Act of 1980 the Federal Reserve lobbied for a change in banking law and was granted the authority under this act to lower the reserve requirement to zero. It was precisely 150 years ago that Karl Marx enumerated in his *Communist Manifesto* ten requirements, or planks, for a successful revolution and a conversion of any country into a socialist state. Plank Number Five reads,

> Centralization of credit in the hands of the state by means of a national bank, the state capital, and an exclusive monopoly.[7]

Since the United States went off the gold standard in 1933, and with its previously giving the Federal Reserve a monopoly on the creation of paper money, this objective for a socialist state has been realized in America for all practical purposes. The bankers at the Federal Reserve constitute its realization.

J.A. Thauberger likens our current situation to that of the gambling industry when he says:

> It is easy to see that no matter how skillfully they play (gamble), eventually the "banker" will end up with all of his original chips back, and except for the very best players, the rest, if they stay in long enough, will lose to the "banker" their homes, their farms, their businesses, perhaps even their cars, watches, rings, and the shirts off their backs (whatever they have mortgaged). Our real life situation is MUCH WORSE than any poker game. In a poker game, none is forced to go into debt, and anyone

can quit at any time and keep whatever he still has. But in real life, even if we borrow little ourselves from the bankers, the local, provincial, and federal governments borrow billions in our name, squander it, then confiscate our earnings from us and pay it back to the bankers with interest. We are forced to play the game and none can leave except by death. We pay as long as we live, and our children pay after we die. If we cannot pay, the same government sends the police to take our property and give it to the bankers. The bankers risk nothing in the game; they just collect their percentage and "win it all." In Las Vegas and at other gambling centers, all games are "rigged" to pay the owner a percentage, and they rake in millions. Canada's monetary system "game" is also rigged and it pays off in billions.[8]

I might add that the U.S. monetary system game is also rigged, and it pays off in the trillions. In the most recent years, these same bankers have added what we might call "authentic" cards to their game.

Credit cards are promoted as a simple convenience and a tremendous boon to trade and commerce. They are actually ingenious devices with which the economic and political elite are getting us used to a cashless society. We are helping to create our own slavery because they make it so convenient.

These same bankers are collecting a 2 to 7 percent discount on every retail sale from the seller and 21 percent in many cases from the buyers. The deck is stacked against the people who choose to play in their system.

Even with the monopoly that the Federal Reserve and banks of the commercial banking system have on the creation of paper money, some banks get reckless and fall victim to their own system. In order to prevent you from having a lack of confidence in their system, they had to devise a scheme to convince you and all others that their system is legitimate, sound and above board — thus, the advent of deposit insurance.

Deposit Insurance

Deposit insurance was never intended to protect depositors. It was intended to protect banks from runs on the bank by depositors. The proof is that, if it were indeed designed to protect depositors, there would never have been a savings and loan crisis. We simply would have closed the bad institutions, paid off depositors from those institutions, and gone about business. However, there was one small problem: There was no money to pay off the depositors.

Deposit insurance and its sole surviving agency, the Federal Deposit Insurance Corporation (FDIC), is not designed to protect you. It is designed to protect bankers from runs on the bank by depositors.

You say, "We have deposit insurance." You have been operating for years under what I call the sticker principal. You see that little gold sticker on the door of most banks, and you take great pride and comfort in the fact that it says, "Your deposits are insured up to $100,000."

The FDIC is a fraud foisted on the American public. Even using their own values in their balance sheet, they can cover, at most, only 0.5 percent of all the deposit fund liabilities they insure.

In past years the FDIC fund, using their own figures, has actually been in the red due to massive bank failures over the past decade. A single failure of one of the major money center banks in New York would more than break the FDIC. When you challenge the FDIC with this fact, they are quick to respond, "Oh, but we are backed by the full faith and credit of the United States Government."

What does that mean in plain English? It means that if the FDIC does not have the money and they must bail out a banking system that has gone under, they will go and borrow the money from the United States Treasury.

Where does the Unites States Treasury get the money? Here we go again — it either has to tax us for it, borrow it, or print it. Either way, you pay for the bailout in any instance. It's a system you cannot leave. It is the heart of power of the economic and political elite who have created a monster that entices you to be a slave to it and the monster system, while making your slavery appear so convenient.

This fact must cause all of us to wonder where are we now in the timeline of things, and what does the future hold?

Chapter 10

STORM CLOUDS OF DISORDER

A s our Lord Jesus Christ instructed us, just as we are able to discern the weather forecast, we must be able to discern the times. There are enormous economic storm clouds popping up on the horizon.

And he said also to the people, When ye see a cloud rise out of the west, straightway ye say, There cometh a shower; and so it is. And when ye see the south wind blow, ye say, There will be heat; and it cometh to pass. Ye hypocrites, ye can discern the face of the sky and of the earth; but how is it that

145

ye do not discern this time? (Luke 12:54-56).

What was once the greatest financial power in the world is now hinged on total economic collapse. Paralyzed by skyrocketing debt, the U.S. government is powerless to protect itself and its citizens from the threat of an impending fallout.

The lobbyist, special interest groups, elected officials and new world order operatives have slowed the engines of spending reform to almost a standstill. The government can't control its own spending in time to prevent a collapse because there is neither the will nor the courage to do what is necessary to change.

By 1996 I believe the interest on the federal debt will exceed the annual personal income tax revenues. As a result, an already devalued currency will lose more ground as the government will have to increase the money supply (printing it) to pay its bills.

Perhaps the most devastating consequence of this economic disorder will be its effect on American citizens. The savings and investments of most Americans will be completely wiped out, leaving them penniless in what would be the worst financial crisis in world history.

But we have a choice. We have an opportunity to protect ourselves and to even prosper in times of economic disorder and turmoil. The opportunity is knowledge — knowledge of how the economic system has grown so fragile and knowledge of the individual components that comprise that system. You must know how simple actions can protect your God-given assets and secure for yourself and your family a more stable economic future. Knowledge will be the key to survival in the financially turbulent years ahead.

Economists and financial forecasters see bleak times ahead for America's economy; contrary to government and media reports, the country is broke and cannot support itself. However, many Americans have the illusion that the federal government will be able to avert a national economic crisis through controls on excessive spending and reforms of government procedures. With so many elected officials under the control and influence of lobbyists, special interest groups and new world order socialists, this probably won't happen in time to prevent a downfall. I was amazed to see in a bulletin distributed by the World Future Society their Forecast Number Five:

> A worldwide economic collapse is extremely likely in the next few years. Those unprepared may stand naked before a crisis unseen in the U.S. since the Civil War.[1]

It wasn't that I was amazed with the information that they were forecasting, because I believe they are absolutely correct. I was amazed that it was they who were forecasting it. The Board of Directors of the World Future Society is made up of such luminaries as Orville L. Freeman, former U.S. Secretary of Agriculture; Sol M. Linowitz, former ambassador to Panama, architect of the Panama Canal giveaway and director of the Marine Midland Bank; Robert S. McNamara, former president of the World Bank and former U.S. Secretary of Defense; Maurice F. Strong, Secretary General, United Nations Conference on Environment and Development; and many others of new world order stature.

It appears in this publication that they're telegraphing a

message to other luminaries that they, too, must get ready for a worldwide economic collapse.

Not only is the collapse likely, it is planned. These people cannot install their new world order without eliminating the strength — economic, political, and otherwise — of any potential resistance to their plans.

The desires of Karl Marx in the *Communist Manifesto* are rapidly being fulfilled, as he called in his fifth plank for a central bank with a monopoly of the mint. This is helping those who would impose this new world order to accomplish their stated goals through the debasement and ruination of the U.S. dollar and our heretofore unquestioned credit.

In order to have worldwide socialism, they must level everybody out and make them equal — equally poor, that is. I can assure you that this process is well under way.

It is a well-known fact that in Japan in the late 1980s the creation of domestic credit exploded; this artificial expansion of money fueled a steep rise in the prices of domestic assets (particularly land and buildings). The soaring value of Japanese real estate provided the collateral against which the Japanese could borrow at home and use the proceeds to buy assets abroad. According to Richard Werner, an economist at Oxford University:

> Since Japan combined this asset price inflation with stable goods prices and an appreciating currency, it achieved a possibly unprecedented feat: through reckless creation of "financial" credit, it printed the means to buy real assets from foreigners. Those foreigners were primarily U.S. citizens who were fleeced, out of ignorance, disinformation, and a system of dishonest weights and measures.[2]

Capital is the means of production. It is the measure of the wealth of a nation. Chart 6 on the next page is one that you have never seen printed in the national media. You probably have never been made aware of the state of economic decline America has fallen into during the 1980s.

This chart shows percentages of world capital by country in 1985 and three years later in 1988. You will note that in just three years, while the Japanese wealth transfer schemes were played out, the U.S. went from having 48.4 percent of the world capital in 1985, to 29.2 percent in 1988. That's a loss of nearly $800 billion in capital in just three years.

During the same period, Japan nearly doubled from 22.5 percent of world capital to 44.2 percent. That's a gain of 21.7 percent of the world capital, or a 96.4 percent increase in their percentage of world capital.

More than $800 billion of wealth was transferred to the Japanese in just three years, with most of it coming from U.S. citizens who are swimming in an ocean of red ink, just struggling to pay back what they owe.

Where Are We Now?

Even with the United States currently being relegated to the status of the largest debtor nation in the world, most people continue to blindly hold instruments of debt (bonds, bills, notes, Federal Reserve notes, CDs and other IOUs) that are at risk of losing their economic, or purchasing, value at anytime.

As previously mentioned, we have more than $12.5 trillion in domestic debt (government, corporate, mortgage and consumer), and only $3.5 trillion in money supply (M-2). When you subtract the $3.5 trillion of money from the $12.5

CHART 6: WORLD CAPITAL

Markets	World Total % 1988	World Total % 1985	Total Cap.[1] (in billions)
Austria	0.1%	0.1%	$4.0
Belgium	0.7	0.5	20.9
Denmark	0.3	0.3	13.0
France	3.0	1.9	78.5
Germany	3.0	4.4	179.0
Italy	1.5	1.6	64.7
Netherlands	1.3	1.3	51.6
Norway	0.2	0.2	9.8
Spain	1.0	0.5	18.7
Sweden	0.9	0.7	29.8
Switzerland	1.5	2.2	90.3
United Kingdom	8.0	8.1	328.3
Total Europe	21.5%	21.8%	$888.6
Australia	1.5	1.5	62.5
Hong Kong	0.8	0.9	38.0
Japan	44.2	22.5	909.1
Singapore/Malaysia	0.5	0.5	20.4
Canada	2.5	3.6	146.7
Mexico	—	0.1	3.4
S. Africa (Gold Mines)	—	0.4	14.7
United States	29.2	48.4	1,955.4
Total World	100.2%	99.7%	$4,038.8

[1] As of December 1985

Columns do not add perfectly due to rounding.

Source: Morgan Stanley Capital International

trillion of debt, you have $9 trillion of the money owed and their debtors who have been asked to do the impossible: Pay back money that doesn't exist.

The flip side of this is that there are $9 trillion that you and many others are holding as loanership assets (notes, bills, bonds, CDs, annuities, etc.) who won't get paid back unless the Federal Reserve prints up more worthless dollars to pay you back. Either way you're going to lose, because if default doesn't wipe you out, inflation will.

Let me drive the point home: There is absolutely no difference between the piece of paper the U.S. Treasury bond is printed on and the paper the Federal Reserve note (what we call dollars) is printed on. Psychologically we look at both of these pieces of paper we are holding and think of them as wealth.

The reality is that the government will never redeem their IOUs because they will never be able to raise taxes high enough to do so. Therefore the U.S. government will perpetually refinance these IOUs as long as anyone will accept these empty promises.

This illusion is temporary and will last only until people holding these and other IOUs (bonds, notes, CDs, money funds) decide it's time to cash in and spend their fortunes. Then, and only then, will the real truth be discovered by the masses.

You must get your financial house in order before panic sets in. It has been said that only when people are about to lose a great amount of their wealth in a fortnight do you have their undivided attention. I hope I have your attention, because beyond the government's debt, we also must consider the economic effects of mortgage, state and local government, business and consumer debt.

Most people are holding a sack full of those IOUs that are tied directly or indirectly to the entire domestic debt of this country. The sad part about all this is that most of these people view their holdings as a sound and secure investment rather than the empty promises they really are.

People are blind to the truth that the government IOUs may never be redeemed and the collateral backing for the private IOUs will vanish the moment the bubble bursts, because most debt securities are intertwined throughout the whole banking and brokerage system. But wait — there's more.

Special Target

If you are approaching the age of 50 or are over 50, you are a special target of the new world order crowd. For those younger, your parents and grandparents are the special targets. Why? Even though those who are 50 years and older comprise only 26 percent of the population in the United States, they are the owners of 80 percent of all money in banks and savings and loans, the holders of 77 percent of the nation's financial assets, and the buyers of 48 percent of all luxury cars.[3]

Fact: This particular age group has been a special target of monetary policy for the past three years. More than three years ago, most of these people who had retired or were relying on their investments to supplement their incomes, were enjoying 8 and 9 percent interest on their CDs and money fund investments.

In late 1991 the Federal Reserve adopted a policy of lower interest rates. The stated goal of the Federal Reserve was to give the economy a shot in the arm with their discretionary monetary policy in order to spur economic activity. There was, however, another goal that was not stated: to transfer wealth from those people who were in the 50-plus age group.

It has been stated by economist after economist that the lowering of interest rates from the period of 1992 through late 1993 has helped the economy to the tune of approximately $25 billion per year. This help to the economy has been for those who have been able to refinance their homes, credit cards and other consumer debt; it has been positive for the economy to the tune of some $25 billion per year.

However, another group that we are not told about — that 50-plus age group that had been depending on their savings for retirement to carry them through their less productive years — were hurt to the tune of approximately $130 billion per year. Instead of earning 8 and 9 percent on their CDs and money funds, they were now earning 2 to 3 percent on those same funds.

They had to cut back their standard of living or start spending their principal. Many of these people, in order to maintain their standard of living, have been dipping into their principal or capital in order to just survive. This has diminished further the income earning ability, as their total asset base is now greatly diminished.

This is just another example of the economic disorder that is upon us. But wait — there's more.

The Real Estate Trap

During the previously mentioned period of lower interest rates, many people refinanced their mortgages, lowered their payments, and in many cases were able to pay more on their principal to accelerate their plans for getting out of debt. This was, and is, good.

During this same period, however, a number of people saw this as the opportunity to move into the home of their dreams. Because of lower interest rates, they were qualified to purchase a more expensive home with perhaps greater living space, a more prestigious address, or perhaps a more modern home with the latest appliances.

Whatever their motive, these people chose to exercise this once-in-a-lifetime opportunity; their incomes hadn't changed, but the lower interest rates allowed them to buy more house since the more expensive homes actually required a lower payment.

But all this has changed. Instead of being able to get a 7 percent loan in mid to late 1993, people were having to pay 8.75 percent for a loan. What does this mean to those home buyers who moved up in the world? If they stay there, pay off their loan and never sell their house, they won't know the difference; but if they need to sell their house, for whatever reason, they have a problem.

The problem is this: A $130,000 mortgage in 1993 at 7 percent interest cost the homeowner $864 a month. The same mortgage in 1994 at 8.75 percent would cost a home buyer $1,022 per month. A potential buyer would have to earn an extra $560 per month to qualify for the $130,000 mortgage in 1994.

I ask the question: How many people can get a $560 per month raise just to qualify for a home loan? Practically none.

What's the dilemma? If you need to sell your house you either won't sell the house or you'll have to lower the price by approximately 12 percent for the potential buyer to qualify. Median income folks sell houses to other median income folks.

As interest rates rise real estate prices will decline; the higher the price, fewer people will qualify for financing at the higher price. You either will be unable to sell your real estate or you will have to lower the price to get it sold. A collapse of the economic and monetary system will only exacerbate the problems for those who are unaware and unprepared for what is coming. But wait — there's more.

The Mutual Fund Trap

Many people are frustrated at receiving only 2-$^1/_2$ to 3-$^1/_2$ percent interest on their CDs, savings and money market funds. After all, with inflation in 1994 running in excess of 5 percent on an annualized basis, we had negative real interest (market rate minus inflation) rates. What do we do with our money?

We have to understand what interest is. Interest is the time-price differential for the use of money and has two factors: risk — whether you will get your money back or not — and inflation — what your money will buy when you get it back. If we are attracted to the promise of higher rates of return on our money, we must evaluate the risk of not getting all or any of our investment money back.

One of the first rules I was taught as a banker was to get my return (interest rate) commensurate with my risk. In today's economic climate, we face the prospect of losing part of our principal due to interest rate risk or market downturn. Today one must be more concerned with return *of* investment than return *on* investment.

What is a mutual fund? Awesome sums of money have been committed to investment in these vehicles called mutual funds, with most of the investors not really understanding what a mutual fund is.

They've been enticed and herded into the mutual fund corral by many well-meaning financial advisors and brokers, helped along by media hype. There appears to be a full choir parroting, "Mutual funds, mutual funds, mutual funds," as a choral response to the question, "Where do I put my money?"

Mutual funds are only a vehicle where investors place their money to be invested in a particular asset. The most common mutual funds are those investing in the stock and bond markets or money market mutual funds.

What most people don't realize is that, more likely than not, your funds have been placed without your full understanding into a stock or bond mutual fund where the risks appear to be the greatest.

A money market mutual fund with check writing privileges offers the least risk (except where they are associated with derivatives). The average maturity of the fixed-rate investments by most funds is usually less than 90 days and offers you liquidity and portability.

Many small investors, tired of low money fund yields and in fear of growing stock volatility, have been jumping into bond funds. At the end of 1992, money invested in bond funds stood at a record $578 billion.

We must not lose sight of the inverse relationship between interest rates and bond prices. As interest rates go up, bond prices come down, causing a loss of capital invested. When we've seen the peak in bond prices (time to sell bonds) and the bottom in interest rates (time to avoid interest rate risk), it is definitely not a time to be buying bonds or investing in bond funds.

High yield bonds (mostly junk), along with long-term government bond funds, offer the greatest rate risk to investors, as the markets are becoming alarmed by the inflation surge.

Astute bond holders deplore inflation because it eats away at the value of the income bonds produce. That again drives bond prices down and yields up. Higher yields make stock dividends less attractive, so stock prices also tend to fall. Those same rising interest rates, poor corporate earnings, higher inflation, and sluggish sales will threaten any bullish or semi-bullish trend that has driven the stock market.

During periods of investor euphoria, many stocks reached valuation levels that looked pretty scary to the more sane investors. When other investors get spooked by rising interest rates and losses, stock fund purchases will be sharply curtailed; you will see some of the more astute investors dumping their stock and bond mutual funds. It is impossible for the markets to continue to rise because there is no demand for stock and bond mutual funds; this predicates a major market decline.

Maybe it's time we stopped listening to the music of the mutual fund parrots and started reading the words and looking at the big picture. The game is rigged and you're about to see one of the most colossal wealth transfer events since 1929. In fact, it's already begun. Writing in the June 16, 1994, edition of *USA Today*, reporter John Waggoner says,

> An increasing number of mutual fund investors are reading their statements, reaching for their phones, and calling their lawyers...many novice investors didn't understand mutual fund risks, but they're finding out now. The average stock fund is down

5.9 percent since the stock market peaked January 31. The average government bond fund has fallen 5.7 percent. Some blame their banks or their brokers.[4]

With bank CD yields hitting an all-time low in 1993, while the average stock mutual fund posted a 13 percent gain, investors poured an estimated $20 billion to $30 billion a month into stock and bond mutual funds, often through banks, brokers or financial planners.

Now investors are shocked that they have lost 5 to 10 percent of their principal, and they want to blame the losses on someone else. Investors' arbitration services usually handle 200 calls a week from irate investors; it is estimated that some 20 percent of those calls are from mutual fund investors. According to William Levine, CEO of Investors Arbitration Services in Woodland Hills, California:

> Calls shot up to 1600 per week in April of 1994; that's a harbinger of future lawsuits.[5]

The interesting part about all this is that this wealth has not been lost; it has merely been transferred. Again, it's the Robin Hood theory that takes from the ignorant and gives to the well-informed who have acted on their information. But wait — there's still more.

Social Security Provides No Security

The facts are in. We'll have fewer workers to support social security in the future, and we'll have more people wanting to enjoy the benefits. I gleaned the following facts from various wire services and U.S. government sources:

- In 1992, Social Security retirement benefit checks were being mailed out at a rate of $29 million per hour around the clock every day of the year, for a total of $254 billion.
- In 1945, there were 41.9 workers for every beneficiary. In 1950, there were 16.5; today, there are 3.2. In the year 2000, there may be fewer than 2.5 workers for every recipient.
- The typical 65-year-old retiree in 1972 earned back all his contributions, plus employer contributions, plus interest on both contributions, in just a little more than two years.
- The Congressional Research Service calculated that the average 1980 retiree got back all they and their employer had paid into the system in just under three years. By 2030, it will take 18 years for the average retiree to make back all they and their employer had paid into the system (this means you'll be paying a lot more or getting a lot less, or both).
- The average monthly benefit for a single worker retiring in 1992 is $794 and $1,191 for a married couple.

The Social Security Trust Fund, by law, is invested in U.S. Treasury securities; our government has been using this money to reduce the stated deficit. It has been loaning to itself your social security retirement funds in the form of zero coupon bonds where the principal and interest come due at the same time, but in the future. Social security is nothing but an economic time bomb waiting to explode. But wait—there's still more to come.

Private Retirement Funds at Risk

We've all heard many people say it sometime: "Oh, I never expect to draw social security." But these same people are definitely expecting to draw from their private pensions, IRAs, Keoghs, 401-Ks or tax-sheltered annuities at some time in the future. I must warn you that these, too, are at risk. Economist Paul Wright, writing in the January 1994 edition of *Monetary and Economic Review*, says,

> Prepare for the beginning of a new "crisis" this year...a crisis affecting some $4 trillion of assets held in public and private pension funds in the United States. Expect Americans' pensions to be confiscated via defaults and public "sacrifice."[6]

The Pension Benefit Guarantee Corporation (PBGC) has estimated that the total underfunding of American pensions has reached approximately $60 billion; if this problem continues, a bailout by the taxpayers may be required.

This $60 billion of private pension woes pales in comparison to the underfunding of the federal military and civilian pension program. The government's unfunded liability to the civilian and military retirees is estimated to be approaching $1.3 trillion.

The unfunded liabilities of these various retirement programs are only part of the problem. The larger part of the problem is where the funded amounts of assets in these pension programs are invested.

Most of those funds in pension programs are invested in a multitude of IOUs (CDs, bonds, annuities, T-bills, notes, mortgages, etc.). These IOUs will either never be repaid or the Federal Reserve will have to print massive amounts of money to pay those liabilities, resulting in a depreciation in the value of the monies that will be coming to the beneficiaries of those retirement funds.

New Kid on the Block

A few years ago, most people had never heard of the term derivative. Derivatives are contracts whose value is linked to price movements in other investments such as stocks, bonds, currencies or commodities. These derivative contracts are highly leveraged instruments, where just a minor market move can mean either great gain or great loss, depending on which side of the movement your derivative contract happens to be linked to.

In recent months, we have seen astronomical losses by heretofore staid and respectable firms of conservative reputation that had ventured out into the derivative market, only to find that great risk awaits most investors when they dabble in this very highly leveraged and volatile market.

USA Today economics reporter James R. Healey wrote that the Paine Webber group injected another $180 million into its short-term U.S. government securities fund because of big losses from risky derivatives. According to Healey, Paine Webber in June of 1994 agreed to spend $88 million to repay some investor losses and buy out some derivatives.[7]

Total for Paine Webber so far appears to be around $268 million, which is the largest reported derivative bailout.

161

Among the other well-known corporate giants that have reported huge derivative losses are Cargill, Inc.; Procter & Gamble; Piper Jaffray Companies; Atlantic Richfield Company; and the Quantum Fund, headed by Wall Street guru George Soros.

Fact: The financial community's involvement in derivatives is so frightening that the Federal Reserve and financial regulators are scared to try to regulate or unwind these firms' involvement in these highly volatile and risky investments. They are afraid to start the unravelling process, because when they do, the whole house of debt cards will collapse.

These derivatives exemplify what's wrong with our economy today: Debt is pledged for more debt, that is pledged to even more debt, and on and on and on. An unwinding of the debt will cause the collapse. It is estimated that the total dollar amount of assets involved in derivatives is between $35 and $40 trillion — equal to three fourths of the value of all stocks, bonds and currencies worldwide.

A triggering event could be a major earthquake or other natural disaster that would destroy confidence in a particular currency or debt issue because of the markets' fear that those obligations could not be repaid. Such an event will begin an unravelling process that ultimately could trigger a worldwide economic collapse.

Banking Crisis

I'm sure most people have been reading as I have the phony PR from the controlled media, claiming that the highly celebrated banking crisis of a few years back has now magically disappeared.

How could it just disappear? It didn't. It is still with us. What we are hearing is the phony PR and reassuring babble coming out of the mouths of central bankers and government officials who are attempting to lull the public to sleep while they're getting ready to do them in.

One of our research staff had analyzed a bank for a reader of *Monetary and Economic Review*, which I publish. This reader had taken action to move money from a weaker bank to one that was stronger. It happened that the weaker bank was a regional bank, its size being in excess of $10 billion. This regional bank was a wholly owned subsidiary of another bank of approximately $100 billion in size.

Our research staffer received a call from a senior officer of the subsidiary bank, complaining because of the C- rating given to their bank. Our staffer explained to the banker that such a rating was fair to weak, which meant that, although we could not recommend the institution, we could not make a strong case that it would immediately incur difficulties. We explained that the bank was currently stable; however, its weaknesses could be magnified during a prolonged period of adverse economic conditions.

Later that same day, I received a conference call from the senior officer of the $10 billion bank, along with a senior executive of the $100 billion parent bank, again complaining about the C- rating given to the subsidiary bank (the subsidiary bank had a very weak liquidity ratio, along with a high percentage of bad loans).

The executive of the parent bank wished to make a point: We should not be concerned about the subsidiary's lack of liquidity because of the subsidiary's line of credit with its parent. His point was that if I wanted to borrow money from you, and you were concerned about my lack of liquidity on my financial statement, you should take great comfort from the fact that my parents (who owe more money than I do) have agreed to loan me some money. Besides, we rated the parent a D+.

You'll be seeing more of these attempts at damage control by multi-billion-dollar regional banks, bank regulators and their lap dogs in the media. They will use such tactics as ridiculing anyone who thinks the system can fail, espousing a "too big to fail" philosophy and giving you reassuring babble that "the government won't let this happen."

The eventual recognition that the mega-bankers' assets are worth much less than the dollar amount of their obligations to their depositors will precipitate a panic and cause the Federal Reserve to inflate the currency at an unprecedented rate. This will cause massive inflation, thus delaying the inevitable depression, the likes of which we have never seen before.

The problem is not found in the banking community alone but spans the entire economy. The government guarantees not only its own borrowings but those of farmers, homeowners, students, the elderly, foreign debtors and anyone else with enough political clout to convince Congress of their special need to be exempted from the disciplines of reality and the marketplace. There is no way to pay these guarantees except to create the money out of thin air.

Even if you have not participated in these examples of government largesse, you and your assets are going to be affected by them if you don't take some defensive action now.

When will it begin? It has begun already. Former FDIC Chairman William Seidman, testifying before the House Budget Committee, said he is seeing "a very worrisome loss of confidence in the U.S. banking industry, and that money is moving out of banks into money market funds, treasury funds, and under mattresses."[8]

Fear causes a run on a bank — fear that is fueled by distrust in not only the banking system, but the economy, federal budget deficits and government leaders. Thomas Jefferson warned us:

> If the American people ever allow private banks to control the issue of their currency, first by inflation, and then by deflation, the banks and the corporations that will grow up around them will deprive the people of all property until their children wake up homeless on the continent their fathers occupied. The issuing power of money should be taken from the banks and restored to Congress and the people to whom it belongs.[9]

U.S. Default: A Possibility

Many economic writers, including myself, have been telling you for years that the safer place for your investments has been Treasury bills. When interest rates are high, we've told you to invest in longer term Treasury bonds and notes. Now I must tell you that even these investments are at risk.

If you had a stack of $100 bills four feet high, you'd be a millionaire. However, you would need a stack 2,600 miles high to pay off what the U.S. government has borrowed and spent on your behalf. Your individual share of the U.S. debt is now approaching $20,000. There is not enough money in the economy to pay off those people who have invested in T-bills, notes and bonds.

Government borrowing to finance current expenditures (budget deficit) now absorbs almost 100 percent of the money available in the economy (net national savings), thereby worsening the economic pressures on private investments.

Meanwhile poverty levels are rising, and approximately 300,000 Americans each week join the unemployment lines. Congress has had to extend unemployment benefits many times each year, which requires the government to spend more for these benefits. Since the government doesn't have the money it must borrow the money, thereby raising the national debt.

When the government borrows this money, it issues T-bills, notes and bonds (IOUs) to anyone who is willing to loan them the money. If you have loaned them the money and are holding T-bills, notes, or bonds, you should be wondering if you'll ever get repaid or even repaid with what?

Part of the American arrogance is the belief, "Default can't happen here. This is America." Almost everyone on Wall Street will tell you that U.S. Treasury securities are risk-free and that the U.S. borrowing capacity to pay you back is unlimited by definition.

As a former banker, I can tell you that the ability of a person, a company or even a government to borrow is predicated on their creditors' confidence in their ability to repay. Foreigners who have been financing much of our expenditures are now getting concerned.

The Social and Economic Congress of Japan has warned Japanese investors that the United States may default on its national debt. That possibility is supported by a report from the General Accounting Office (GAO), the auditing arm of the Congress. The report hints that the U.S. economy will shrink 40 percent in the next 20 years if the country continues its approach to budgeting and spending.

Our failure to reverse those trends in fiscal policy and the way we spend money at the federal level will doom future generations to a stagnating standard of living, damage U.S. competitiveness and influence in the world, and hamper our ability to address pressing national needs. This is exactly the place where the new world order gurus want us.

Any banker in his right mind would not loan money to anyone in the condition I have just described. This begs the question, "Should you loan money to anyone in this financial condition?"

You may be asking right now, "What will the government do?" Frankly, there is no way out of this economic mess, short of default. The question is will the default occur all at once or on the installment plan? I expect the government one day to say what a number of foreign governments have told their creditors: "We can't afford to pay you any more."

"Unthinkable!" you say. "This can't happen in America!" It will happen, and the only thing I believe that is being debated in the inner circles of the government and the Federal Reserve is how and when this event of default will occur.

I was quite surprised to read in the *Washington Post* an article entitled, "With Debt Burgeoning, Could the U.S. Default?" You have to understand that the *Washington Post* is the flagship political newspaper of the powerful establishment press in the United States. It is significant that they are tossing forth the idea of a possible default. The article touts a plan by former Federal Reserve official R. Christopher Whalen, who says:

Defaulting is preferable to a long, painful slide that will only postpone the day when the United States returns to economic and financial health. By doing it now, the nation could swallow all the bitter medicine in one big gulp and get on with rebuilding.

Let's just admit the reality that the national debt will never be repaid or that it will be repaid in inflated dollars and start over. [10]

You must be asking the question, "How would a default work?" According to the former Federal Reserve analyst, "The government could announce that it would no longer pay interest to holders of U.S. Treasury bills, notes and bonds. Then the Federal Reserve bank system could agree to buy back all these securities at their face value. [11]

To do this, the Federal Reserve would have to print as much as another $5 trillion to redeem all of the debt owed by the government. Such a measure would be devastating to most in the economy who never suspected such a thing could ever happen. The printing or creating of billions of new dollars would, in the short term, cause unprecedented inflation. Whalen says further:

In short, the risk of economic turmoil would be outweighed by action that would wake up the nation and tell taxpayers what the story is. The only way politicians have gotten away with this is that the consequences of old borrowing have come out in dribs and drabs. If the government doesn't move soon for an orderly reduction of debt, we're headed for a repudiation of interest.

It'll be third world economics time. We would
destroy a lot of wealth. It would put us in the ranks
of Brazil. [12]

The fact is, wealth won't be destroyed as Mr. Whalen says;
it will be transferred to those who understand what's happening and take definitive steps to protect their assets. Everyone
who is concerned about their financial well-being must
change their thinking and misconceptions about how this system really works.

Most people's minds are blocked to the truth about the
corruption and imminent collapse of our system because they
think, "It has always worked that way; nothing like this has
ever happened here in America."

If you're fearful of changing your thinking, let me assure
you that you have a choice: You can change your investment
strategies or get ready to change your lifestyle after you get
wiped out. The storm clouds of disorder are clearly visible on
the horizon, a sure indicator of the storm that is rapidly
approaching.

Is there anything we can do to protect ourselves? Yes, there
is, and I'll cover those specifics in a later chapter. But first, let's
examine a major road block the insiders have placed in our
paths.

Chapter 11

FINANCIAL PRIVACY AND THE CASHLESS SOCIETY

There is a point that I must drive home even at the risk of being repetitive: Life as we have known it in the United States is about to change and change drastically. You should not fear, though, because our God is not a God of fear. At the same time I do not believe it is God's desire that we remain ignorant of the things going on around us. God points out many times that we should get wisdom and understanding.

As we read God's Word carefully each day we see that He has a plan to deliver His people from this present evil age and world order. However, there are road blocks along the way as we travel that path God has set for each one of us. The major road blocks we are facing in these times are the goals of the new world order.

Over the past two decades, I have dedicated much of my adult life to the study of the books, publications, papers and documents of the organizations connected with and promoting a new world order. I believe that I can summarize for you their primary goals as being in six major areas:

• Abolish ordered government.

This must be accomplished in order that they can super-impose their supra-national government upon the rest of the world, including the United States. A recent example was the passing of the North American Free Trade Agreement, promoted as an agreement and document for free trade.

Let me assure you that NAFTA has nothing to do with free trade. If you and I are going to enter into a free trade agreement, do we need a 5,000-7,000 page document to accomplish that? The answer is obvious.

NAFTA was simply the mechanism setting up kingdom number one of the ten kingdoms of the new world order. This document, much of it still secret, overrules and overrides the sovereign documents of our nation, including our Constitution.

• Eliminate private property.

This is most essential for the new world order crowd if they are to crush any resistance to their plans. Without private property, you must go to the state for your resources and sustenance. This is a blatant attempt to replace God on the throne as our provider.

- Eliminate inheritance.

They must eliminate the passing of property to children and grandchildren; the owning of private property gives you the resources and the power to resist their actions. They want to control the economic and social behavior of everybody.

One of the ways they will eliminate inheritance is through legislation eliminating any exemptions from inheritance taxes. Expect inheritance taxes to become confiscatory.

- Abolish patriotism.

This must be accomplished because your allegiance and patriotic duty to a sovereign nation is totally unacceptable to the promoters of the new world order. Their desire is to tear down the present sovereign boundaries of nations and replace them with new boundaries drawn by the establishment elite.

William Wood, the chief geographer for the State Department of the United States, said:

> What we are dealing with is the re-creation of countries. [1]

Julian Minghi, the U.S. representative to the International Geographical Union, said:

> The notion of boundaries as we've known them, in terms of absolute sovereignty and legalities, will, in time, dwindle.
>
> A stratified system of government and power is likely to replace traditional states; at the top will be a stronger United Nations, or an equivalent body responsible for peace, environmental, and other global issues. [2]

- Rid the world of all religion.

That is, rid it of all religion except theirs. And what is theirs? Theirs will be a religion that will control the minds of men — New Age pantheism — which says that there is a god force in everything; therefore Mother Earth, animals and men are gods.

> Who changed the truth of God into a lie, and worshipped and served the creature more than the Creator (Rom. 1:25).

> Having a form of godliness, but denying the power thereof: from such turn away (2 Tim. 3:5).

- Destroy the family unit.

This is perhaps the most evident of all of the activities of the new world order. We are seeing outright assaults on every aspect of the family unit — the system that God designed to be the stabilizing force and the basic unit of how we dwell together here on this earth.

The cornerstone of this diabolical plan is to attack the family unit by making the children subservient to, and wards of, the state. This plan has advanced so far that children in a traditional family setting are now considered to be at risk, thereby subject to being taken out of the home by the social planners of the state.

Why Worry About Privacy?

Writing in *Monetary and Economic Review,* former White House aide Charles E. Bates says:

Personal privacy has always been of the utmost importance to people. In this "age of information," it is becoming increasingly difficult to maintain privacy, whether it be personal or financial. Every day, millions of Americans are either coerced or simply duped into divulging very personal information about themselves. The invaders of privacy attack from many different angles, in an attempt to learn everything there is to know about you and your family. [3]

With that statement in mind, we must be concerned about oppressive government intrusion. In the quest to establish the new world order, the elitists want to eliminate any assets that would allow you to be a resistance force to their plans.

They will eliminate your personal assets through a myriad of obscure provisions of the various laws, including the Crime Control Act of 1994.

These obscure provisions simply allow police state tactics to confiscate property without due process. This is done under a clever theory of law that the "property committed the crime, and therefore, the property has no rights." This power grab is running rampant all across the nation.

One also has to worry about privacy because of harm, or potential harm, to their reputation. For example, you may make a financial contribution to, be a member of, or support a group that is labeled by the press as being politically incorrect. Your support, particularly if you are somewhat of a public figure or outspoken person, in ministry or otherwise, may result in someone targeting you with a propaganda campaign.

And there are always the divorce lawsuits, family disputes, etc., that a potential adversary may attempt to use (through litigation or other adversarial proceedings) in attacking your strong stand on a particular issue.

Then there's the issue of security: personal as well as security of your property. It is a well-known fact that the greatest part of security is secrecy.

Finally, you must worry about privacy because of political, religious or racial persecution. What used to be the "land of the free and the home of the brave" is now being folded in as just another division of the new world order.

The Major Road Block

Economist Norman N. Franz says:

> Naturally, the major key to worldwide political control will be to create a closed financial and monetary system that will besiege the whole world. Article 8, Section G of the *Constitution for the Federation of Earth* creates the world financial administration that will be empowered to "establish and operate a planetary banking system, making transition to a common global currency (called earth dollars)...to establish and implement the procedures of a planetary monetary and credit...and to establish and operate the procedures for the collection of revenues (taxes) for the world government." This is significant because they plan to use this closed financial system to enforce their new brand of world law. [4]

In order to enforce this new brand of world law that Norman Franz refers to, there must be an enforcement network. As a part of their thrust to monitor and control the American people, the U.S. government has established a prototype for the rest of the world called the Financial Crimes Enforcement Network (FINCEN) that is located in Arlington, Virginia.

Through the use of highly sophisticated computers our own government has combined more than a hundred data bases on bank records, driving records, census data, criminal suspects and myriads of business and financial activities of millions of honest, law-abiding citizens.

FINCEN is the largest government-run artificial intelligence data base ever established. It has more than 300 employees from the IRS, FBI, Secret Service, FDIC, BATF, CIA and DIA (Defense Intelligence Agency). This network acts as a collection point, clearing house and distribution center of computerized data for almost all other government agencies. Their source of data comes from federal bank regulators' reports, bank deposits, census income figures, Secret Service, credit reports, FBI and DEA drug data and even Customs Service reports.

It is estimated that FINCEN currently has access to more than forty financial data bases and another 100 are being created. These include computerized land records, credit reports, real estate transfer records, Form 8300 Currency Reports, bank reports of large currency transactions, etc. I understand from reliable sources that the data, financial patterns, models and individual names generated by FINCEN are being shared with a myriad of other government agencies.

FINCEN and U.S. government officials admit that FINCEN is a trial run for a world system of financial tracking, surveillance and control. FINCEN, or whatever name they wish to call it, is a most essential element for the implementation of their new world order.

You wonder what records are kept. The following is just a partial list of the sources of information about you and your lifestyle that may be in the hands of other people:

- Social security
- Federal, state and local tax returns
- School records
- Birth, marriage, and death certificates
- Court records
- Passport records
- Census records
- Bank records
- Motor vehicle licenses and registrations
- Medical histories
- Unemployment compensation
- FBI and police records
- Insurance companies
- Car dealers' records
- Mortgage companies' records
- Mail-order firm records
- Clubs and organizations
- Genealogical bureaus
- Churches
- Magazines and other publications

The Cashless Society

We are well on our way toward a cashless society. A major

super highway is being built to accomplish this goal. That super highway is none other than the information super highway announced in early 1994 by Vice President Al Gore. This information super highway may have many seemingly attractive features, but I can assure you its main feature will be to enslave you and control your economic and social behavior, right from the TV screen in your own home. Writing in *Unravelling the New World Order*, economist Norman Franz says:

> Currently, there is a move toward a cashless society that is being facilitated by the emergence of the "smart card." The smart card of the future has a computer chip that can store any and all information pertaining to an individual's life. This includes his/her description, address, birth date, social security number, blood type, occupation and work place. Financially, it will contain all your bank account and investments balances; and all transactions and corresponding changes in account balances will be limited to only those who have the card. [5]

Franz goes on to say:

> Technology currently exists where this type of computer chip has been successfully implanted under the skin of a person's hand and/or forehead. [6]

I believe that we must all ask ourselves if we living in the times where a world ruler will do as prophesied in Revelation 13:16-17:

And he causeth all, both small and great, rich and poor, free and bond, to receive a mark in their right hand, or in their foreheads: and that no man might buy or sell, save he that had the mark, or the name of the beast, or the number of his name.

With the advent of the smart card and now a newly designed U.S. currency, it appears that the answer to that question is an emphatic yes.

I firmly believe that we are living in the last days that are outlined by the apostle John in the Book of Revelation. If that is the case, we must get our own houses in order, spiritually and financially, if we are going to be effective in doing the work that God has called each and every one of us to do during this time.

Hence, one of the major tools that Satan uses to accomplish his purposes is money. This means that we must get our financial house in order so that we will not be taken down with the system as it collapses into a major state of disorder.

What, then, can we do? I'll cover that in the following chapter.

Chapter 12

WEALTH TRANSFER
AND ASSET ALLOCATION

Will You Survive?

Permit me to repeat what I said in the introduction to this book: The greatest shock of this decade is that more people are about to lose more money than at any time before in our history. But the second greatest shock will be the incredible amount of money just a relatively small group of people will make at exactly the same time.

You have a choice. You can either sit there and let them dish it out to you, or you can do something about it. If you insist on just sitting there, believing the disinformation from government officials, the Federal Reserve, economists at brokerage houses and banks and the mainstream press, you will watch most of your traditional investments end up in the graveyard of capital.

"Pretty strong words!" you say. Yes, they are. Quite frankly, I have neither the time nor the inclination to beat around the bush on this issue. Our economy is in serious trouble. You know it and I know it. Your debt-related or loan-ership type of investments are about to get in trouble — deep, deep trouble.

The Hoax

"How so?" you may ask. Politicians and many Wall Street economists continue to boast about how we have entered a new era in global economics. They subsequently have declared the old laws of economics to be dead. They tell us that we are entering a new era of prosperity, engineered by monetary policy decisions, complete with central bank coordination; over the long haul we can be assured of lower interest rates, stable prices and prosperity for everybody.

Most people buy this rhetoric; therein lies the foundation for your greatest financial opportunity in sixty years. For centuries, politicians and central bankers have conspired to create an illusion of prosperity through debt and money creation. An example of that is the following chart which shows the history of the federal debt from 1913 and projected at the same rate of growth to the year 2000.

Most agree that the federal government will never pay off the debt, because it is impossible. They will simply roll over the debt and the interest due on that debt year after year. Therefore, by definition, irredeemable IOUs and printing press money are fraud.

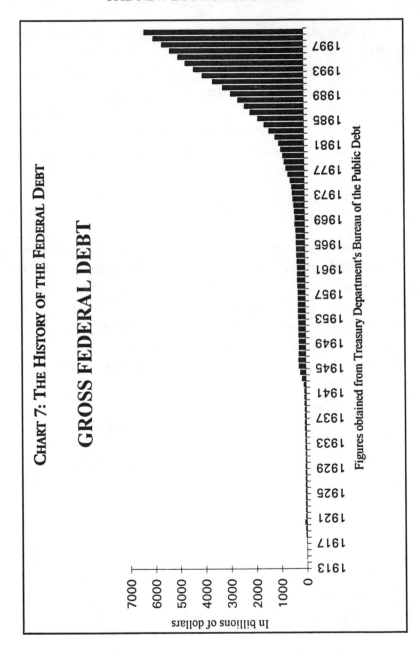

CHART 7: THE HISTORY OF THE FEDERAL DEBT

GROSS FEDERAL DEBT

Figures obtained from Treasury Department's Bureau of the Public Debt

In billions of dollars

Every nation that has followed this course of mounting debt and the illusion of prosperity has suffered dire consequences. The euphoria brought on by its phony purchasing power quickly evaporates as the new debt is purged from the economy through either default or depression, or through inflation and depreciation. Throughout history there have been no exceptions, and there have been no soft landings.

How, then, can we explain this phenomenon? If money creation causes inflation, how is it possible that the debt and money supply could have expanded with such ferocity over the past eight years without touching off a surge in price inflation and a resultant depression? Have government officials and central bankers discovered a new secret for continued "printing press prosperity" without an economic price being paid for our largesse?

As astounding as it seems, that's what most people believe. A client told me the other day, "Look, we've printed money, increased our debt, and nothing has happened." That's right — not yet.

Economic Time Bomb

We currently are sitting on an economic time bomb that can explode any day. Common sense must tell you that something is drastically wrong. The alchemy of ancient days does not work; it is not possible to slap ink on paper, call it a Federal Reserve note and have it turn into gold. Yet that is what insiders (central bankers, politicians and media moguls) are trying to convince you has happened. This is the big lie that most people have swallowed.

This economic time bomb is ticking away; its explosion

will mean either great loss or great fortune to you. To profit from this, however, you must first dispel the misconceptions you have about how the economy and investments work, because there is a herd mentality in the market place that guides millions of savers and investors, both large and small.

They are simply mesmerized by the reassuring babble of so-called experts and have greedily continued to accumulate paper IOUs in the form of Treasury bonds, municipal bonds, corporate bonds, certificates of deposits, money funds and, more recently, derivative contracts — part of an ever-widening spectrum of debt securities.

The sad part about all of this is that these people view their holdings as conservative, sound and secure investments rather than the empty promises that they are. They are blind to the obvious truth that the government IOUs and even private IOUs may never be redeemed. The collateral backing for the private IOUs will simply vanish the moment the bubble bursts, because most debt securities are interrelated and intertwined throughout the whole banking and brokerage system.

The Seductive Trap

I suppose the cruelest financial indicator of all for the unsuspecting is immediate past performance. Not only is it the cruelest, it is perhaps the most dangerous and misleading indicator influencing the decisions of most investors.

Ron Wilson, a friend and financial advisor, told me one day, "Larry, most people when they decide to make an investment will go to the supermarket or newsstand and pick up *Money* magazine or some other mainstream publication. They will pore over the pages of advertisements for mutual funds and other investments, then pick up the phone, call all of the 1-800 numbers they found in the magazine, and request their financial information. Then for weeks the UPS driver brings package after package that ends up on the dining room table. Finally, one day the investor and spouse sit down, open all of the packages of information, pore over the details and then make their decision, based on that cruel indicator called 'immediate past performance.'"

Their investment is selected because it has been sold to them as a good investment, it has gone up, and people have made money on it. This may well have been an investment where the last ones to buy are the first ones to lose money because astute investors, who got in early at a lower price, decided to sell and take their profits.

There are generally three types of investors: winners, losers and game players. If you're going to survive in these economic times, you must buy things (investments) when nobody wants them, and you should sell those same investments when everybody wants them.

Misguided Advice

Many times individuals have made decisions on asset allocation based on the advice of financial planners. In many cases, these financial planners are Christians and are giving the individuals the best advice they know, with no malice or deceit on their part. They simply don't know any better because, in many cases, the misguided advice is based on a world view instead of reality as it exists.

Many investors and their financial advisers fall into the trap of not understanding our monetary system and are carried with the rest of the herd down the path to financial destruction.

Many people do not know what money is and what money is not. They do not realize that in this country and around the world we have a discretionary monetary economy, which means that, at the discretion of the monetary policy-makers (the Federal Reserve), some investments will prosper while other investments will end up in the graveyard of capital.

Unfortunately, many well-meaning investment advisors, financial planners and investors themselves will simply deal at the level of investment vehicles and never consider the underlying factor that determines the well-being of those investments. That factor is the monetary system.

It is very much like to a person being concerned about a growing plant: They are constantly viewing, carrying for, trimming the leaves and the blooms on a nice plant. While they are doing this, they have not concerned themselves with the root system. You can have the most beautiful plant in the world, and you can do a marvelous job of trimming and caring for that plant. But if you don't understand the root system your plant may die, and you may never know why.

The same principle applies to your investments. Your investment may end up in the graveyard of capital and you may never know why, if you don't understand the monetary system. Many people concern themselves with return *on* investments when they should be more concerned with return *of* investments.

Interest is probably one of the most misunderstood factors of the economic world. Interest is the time/price differential for the use of money; it has two factors: risk — whether you will get your money back or not — and inflation — what will

CHART 8: THE COST OF INFLATION

Annual Investment Return Required to Break Even

If inflation is...		5%	7.5%	10%	12.5%	15%	17.5%	20%
	0%	5.0%	7.5%	10.0%	12.5%	15.0%	17.5%	20.0%
and your	15%	5.9%	8.8%	11.8%	14.7%	17.6%	20.6%	23.5%
tax bracket	28%	6.9%	10.4%	13.9%	17.4%	20.8%	24.3%	27.8%
is...	31%	7.2%	10.9%	14.5%	18.1%	21.7%	25.4%	29.0%

For example, if inflation is 10% and you are in the 28% tax bracket, your money must have an annual 13.9 rate of return in order to retain its purchasing power.

your money buy for you when you get it back. A person must get their yield commensurate with their risk.

This was one of the first rules I was taught as a young banker: "Get your yield commensurate with your risk." A risk involves not only whether you're going to get your money back, but it involves what your money will buy for you when you get it back. Chart 8 on the preceding page shows you the cost of inflation and the annual investment return required just to break even, based on your tax bracket.

State of Your Flocks

The Bible tells us that we should be careful to "know the state of [our] flocks" (Prov. 27:23). In other words, we should be aware of the location and the condition of our God-given assets at all times. In order to help us understand the state of our financial flocks, we must understand that there are only two types of assets in a modern economy: loanership assets or ownership assets, or a combination of both.

The following chart helps us to see the contrast between the two different types of assets.

Chart 9		
Ownership	vs.	Loanership
Gold		FRNs
Silver		MM Funds
Platinum		CDs
Coins		T–Bills
Stocks		Annuities
Real Estate		Bonds
Collectibles		Notes

I have listed them in both the ownership and the loaner-ship columns in order of declining liquidity. It is important for us to understand the need for liquidity, because during times of economic turmoil there is always a flight to cash.

Let's review the various assets in the loanership column. Everything in this column is nothing but an IOU. Each is a promise to pay; in each investment you are dependent upon someone else's performance in paying you back. They are listed in the order of liquidity; let's review them one by one:

FRNs (or Federal Reserve notes) — These are what we carry in our wallets and refer to as dollars. But, as I mentioned previously, they are not dollars; they are simply "IOU nothings" issued by a private bank and forced upon us by the legal tender laws. In the not-too-distant future they may become extinct, replaced by a smart card in a cashless society.

Money Market Funds — These are funds that invest in short-term debt instruments such as overnight repurchase agreements, CDs, T-bills, bonds, commercial paper, notes, etc. with an average maturity of less than ninety days. This tends to eliminate the interest rate risk on these funds. Lately a heretofore unknown risk in the form of derivatives has attached itself to these funds.

CDs — These are certificates of deposits issued by banks. They can be issued for short periods of time or longer periods of time. In a period of rising interest rates, it is to one's advantage to invest only for shorter periods of time. It is also incumbent upon the investors to know the condition of the banks to which they are loaning their money.

T-Bills — These are short-term debt instruments issued by the U.S. Treasury which previously have been considered an excellent short-term parking place for your money. With the looming prospect of the U.S. government's default, one must keep a wary eye on this instrument as an investment.

Annuities — Annuities can only be issued by insurance companies. In the case of an annuity, you have simply loaned your money to the insurance company. As a financial intermediary, the insurance company turns around and loans it out to other people and entities. Once again you must know the financial condition of the insurance company to which you have loaned your money in order to determine their ability to honor their commitment to you. Many of the insurance companies that appear sound at this time will not be able to perform and redeem the IOU that you are holding simply because the people they have loaned your money to will be unable to redeem their IOUs when economic disorder sets in.

Bonds — Bonds may be issued by federal, state, county and municipal governments or corporations. These instruments, again, are nothing but IOUs; while governments that have issued general obligation type bonds have taxing power to raise the money to redeem the bonds and pay you back, a period of economic disorder may cause governments at every level to default on their obligations. We already have seen that same situation occur in the corporate sector where many bonds issued by corporations turn to junk and became unmarketable. If you find yourself holding bonds that are unmarketable, this means you will not be able to redeem them for cash.

Notes — Notes may be issued by governments, corporations or individuals. These instruments are generally intermediate or even long term as it relates to maturity. Again, they are an IOU or a promise to pay. In holding a note, one must consider the collateral, if any, that is backing the note that you are holding. Since the note is an IOU, you always must be aware of the credit worthiness of the entity or individual to whom you have loaned your money. You have to be constantly aware of their ability to repay. Their ability to repay may be hampered by events beyond their control during periods of economic disorder.

Sadly, most people holding these loanership assets view them as sound and secure investments rather than the empty promises they are. They are blind to the obvious truth that the government IOUs may never be redeemed and the collateral backing for the private IOUs will simply vanish the moment the bubble bursts.

If you persist, in the face of the obvious economic disorder that is upon us, in holding onto your loanership assets, be advised that these debt securities carry a double risk: the risk of default in the event of recession/depression and the risk of capital depreciation in the event of accelerating inflation.

In other words, in the coming months, if the first one doesn't wipe you out, the second one will. So what do we do? For those who understand the monetary system, it is obvious that in periods of depreciating or potentially depreciating currencies, you begin to move assets from loanership to ownership. Ownership assets are properties that are not someone else's liability.

Let's examine each one of those assets in the ownership category:

Gold — Gold is money, and money is gold. God designed it that way, and that's the way it is. If you go back and review Chapter 7 regarding commercial Babylon and check the characteristics of money, you will see the reason that gold is money and money is gold.

Since we have economic and political insiders attempting to decide our future, we have to be cognizant of owning the right kind of gold. In 1933, President Franklin D. Roosevelt stole the citizens' gold under Executive Order #6102 by having them surrender their gold to the Federal Reserve who, in return, gave them worthless IOUs for their gold.

We had gold confiscation then and we will have gold confiscation again. Section II(B) exempts certain coins because of their numismatic value; therefore, one should be holding semi-numismatic or rare coins in gold in order that they would be exempted from another confiscation by the government.

I know some are saying, "They can just change the law." That's right. But why do you suppose they put the exemption there to begin with? It was to protect the insiders' holdings from confiscation. The economic and political elite always will leave themselves an exit to be used when the crisis comes. We simply must be as smart as they are and locate the exits ahead of time.

Silver — Silver is not only a monetary metal, but it is also an industrial metal.

Silver has been referred to as the poor man's gold because of its lower price per ounce in relation to the price of gold. Up until 1965, our dimes, quarters and half dollars all contained 90 percent silver by content.

A person who in 1965 had set aside a $1,000 face value amount of silver coins, be it in dimes, quarters or halves, found that by mid-1994 that same $1,000 face value was worth more than $4,000. Those pre-1965 dimes, quarters and halves are not worth any more today than they were in 1964...your paper money is just worth less.

Gold and silver always have been the money of the Bible. It still remains the money of the Bible regardless of what the world view might say. The most common fallacy that has been promoted regarding gold and silver is that gold and silver should be avoided because they're too volatile in price. When I hear someone make that statement, I know they haven't a clue as to how this entire monetary system of ours works. They have been captured by the world system and mesmerized by its psychological money.

Paper currencies are simply boats on the ocean of the economy, and they are all sinking. Some just happen to be sinking faster than others. There is the source of your volatility. Gold and silver are stable; it's the currencies that are volatile.

John Evans, a reporter for the London-based *The European* newspaper writes,

> Central bankers in Europe and the U.S. say they are becoming alarmed by a dramatic rise in foreign exchange trading which has quadrupled in two years to reach $5 trillion a day. Trading figures derived by estimates collected by central banks ahead of a major survey to be published next year were described last week by regulatory sources as, "an orgy of dangerous over-trading."

Evans continues,

> Central bankers privately admit that markets risk

recreating the crisis which hit Bankhaus Herstatt 20 years ago when regulators shut down a small German bank running several billions of dollars of currency transactions, causing massive disruption and liquidity shortfalls in the international banking system. [1]

One simple fact remains: Governments can't print silver and gold, and that speaks volumes.

Platinum — Although being a very precious metal and perhaps the most precious metal, platinum has not been used as widely as a monetary metal as silver and gold have been but is being acquired by investors around the world in legal tender coin form. Platinum also has been referred to by many people as the environmental metal; you cannot have a single gallon of gasoline or have clean air or clean water without the use of the catalytic properties of platinum.

The current supply of platinum is so thin that annual mining producton is snapped up by industrial users and a small but increasing number of investors who have discovered a potential for profit in buying this metal.

Because more than 80 percent of the supply of this metal comes from South Africa, a nation in political turmoil, it is in great question as to whether a steady supply of platinum will be available to the industrialized world in the next few years. Again, platinum is an ownership assets in a highly liquid and marketable state.

Coins — Here we are referring to what are known as rare coins. These are coins with a higher percentage of numismatic or collector value than the actual value of the coin's bullion content.

The value of these coins is determined, as in any investment, by the demand for them. In addition to demand, the value of rare coins is determined by the age of the coin, the condition of the coin, and the known population of the coin. A coin that is scarce, meaning having a low population with a high mint state or condition, will have greater value than a coin that is plentiful and has been circulated.

The acquisition and holding of rare coins has been the hobby of kings and rulers for centuries.

Stocks — Stocks are simply pieces of paper that evidence your share of ownership in a corporation. Stocks are ownership assets; however, they are different from all other ownership assets because the stock certificate has no intrinsic value in and of itself. It merely is a security that has been issued to you in return for your investment of equity in a company. This is just another market where the money manipulators and their political enforcers rushed in and created themselves a monopoly in the trading of these securities.

This system opened up whole new avenues for market manipulation and wealth transfer. It now has become so sophisticated that new instruments such as mutual funds were designed; masses of sheep (small investors) were herded into these markets to be fleeced or sheared at will.

This is another example of how commercial Babylon, complete with its banking monopoly, has used a market for manipulation and as a massive wealth transfer mechanism. They were able to do this only after they had acquired the monopoly on creation of paper money. Until that time, it was an honest and legitimate market.

Real Estate — Real estate is an ownership asset. It is, however, a very localized investment because the value of real estate is dependent on many factors, many of them having to do with the economy of the geographic location of the particular parcel of real estate.

From an overall economic perspective, real estate is most dependent upon interest rates since most buyers of real estate must have access to credit at a reasonable rate. A rise in the general level of interest rates will cause a downturn in the economy and also will increase the cost of funds, thereby negatively impacting the value of real estate.

This is a market where one must do an inordinate amount of due diligence before purchasing real estate in a particular market. The same is true if you want to market real estate holdings, as the most ideal time to sell real estate is when the general level of interest rates is low.

Real estate has a disadvantage in that it is one investment that governments could eventually confiscate by merely raising the tax rates to confiscatory levels. Because of its general lack of liquidity, one should carefully weigh the percentage of assets they are holding in the area of real estate.

Collectibles — Collectibles are items such as art, oriental rugs, Chinese vases, ceramics, etc. These items are truly ownership, but they are probably the least liquid of all ownership assets. An investor must understand the market in what he is buying in this area and always raise the question, "Where can I sell the item if I should need to liquidate it?" I do not recommend collectibles as a viable investment option.

There you have it. Here's your choice: ownership verses loanership. I must emphasize again that in periods of economic uncertainty and potential economic disorder, it is wise to be liquid. There's a saying that always has held true, "Cash at the crash will be king."

Looking back at all of the different options and choices for the allocation of assets, we again ask, "What, then, must we do?"

To get a valid answer, we always must go to God's Word.

Cast thy bread upon the waters: for thou shalt find it after many days. Give a portion to seven, and also to eight; for thou knowest not what evil shall be upon the earth (Eccl. 11:1-2).

What the scripture is saying is that in "casting our bread upon the waters" we are to be bold in our investments and asset allocation. In verse 2 we are instructed to diversify, because we do not know precisely when the evil and calamity will fall upon the earth.

Wisdom and prudence dictate that we discern the times in which we're living. These times are times of economic disorder because man has outsmarted himself; in his arrogance and ignorance he has tried to operate contrary to God's economy, and the consequences are going to be disastrous.

If the general population understood the fundamentals of real money that you and I now realize, they would soon refuse to accept the U.S. dollar or any paper currency or other security tied to it for and would demand payment in gold and silver.

In order to come out of the world system and have a bit of economic insurance, one should have a minimum of 30 percent of their assets in the precious metals. This percentage will rise as events become more ominous. One needs the precious metals, because they are the only monetary assets that are not someone else's liabilities. I believe that in the not too distant future many of us will be using the honest money of precious metals for our medium of exchange; we may be forced out of the world's monetary system because we refuse to bow down and be a part of their abominable system.

The money manipulators and their political enforcers are in a box. They have run out of options, because if they stop debauching (printing) the currency, the game is over. Everything will come to a screeching halt and people will come to the rude awakening and understanding of the massive fraud that has been foisted on them for the past several decades.

Remember, debauching the currency is the economic equivalent of smoking crack cocaine: you get high for a while, but in the end it wipes you out.

Most Americans have become slaves to the creators of psychological money; however, it's not mandatory that you remain a slave on their plantation. By taking appropriate actions now, you can prosper from your knowledge of the system. Unfortunately, most will struggle to survive.

You have a choice. That's the way it's been throughout history: people making choices. As children of God we have but one choice, and that is to follow His instructions as they relate to every aspect of our lives — and that includes economics. God, through the apostle John in the book of Revelation, has warned us about mystery Babylon — that demonic blend of economics, politics and religion. He has given strict instructions for His children:

> And I heard another voice from heaven, saying, Come out of her, my people, that ye be not partakers of her sins, and that ye receive not of her plagues (Rev. 18:4).

Chapter 13

THE JOSEPH GENERATION

In the Old Testament God raised up a people to be a light to those in Satan's dark world. These people, chosen to represent God, were called the children of Israel.

Throughout the ages, God has shown through His Holy Word that He has a will, a purpose and a plan to deliver His people from the hand of the enemy. It was true during the times recorded in the Bible, and it is still true today.

God sovereignly saved the children of Israel from starvation and ultimate extinction during the times of famine and economic disorder by raising up Joseph to a position where he could not only meet their temporal needs, but minister to their spiritual needs as well.

God does, indeed, have a plan. I believe God is saying that He raises up such people today: people He has found faithful in every aspect of their lives; people who have the heart of David and the spirit of Moses, Joshua and Caleb; people who have read the back of the book and know that we win; people who have been found faithful in the little things. Now God is ready to enlarge their tent stakes and make them rulers over greater things.

It is obvious a wealth transfer is coming. God has promised that the wealth of the wicked is going to be given to the righteous. God's Word is going to go forth throughout all the earth, and in order to get the message out, finances will be needed.

I firmly believe this generation of Josephs God is raising up will be the recipients of the end-time transfer of wealth. They are a people who "hath an ear to hear" what the spirit of the true and living God is saying to the churches in these last days.

There are people who have cried out for wisdom and understanding of the times. They are a people, described by Pastor Randel McCarty, who "see it, say it and seize it," in that they see the vision God has, not only for the church, but for themselves individually. They are not afraid to say what God has put on their hearts. They seize the moment of opportunity — the opportunity, as Pastor McCarty said, that separates the "concerned" from the "committed." [1]

Rejoice, saints of God, because victory is ours in Jesus' name!

Notes

Introduction
1. *Patrick Henry — Life, Correspondence and Speeches* by William Wirt Henry, Volume I, Bert Franklin, New York, Oris Pub. 1891, Reprinted 1969.

Chapter 1 — Understanding the Times
1. *Wall Street Journal,* 17 December 1992, p. 1.

Chapter 2 — God's Promises
1. *Personal Worker's Testament* (Philadelphia: National Publishing Company, 1968), p. A5-6.
2. Frederic Bastiat, *The Law* (Irvington-on-Hudson, N.Y.: The Foundation for Economic Education, 1950), pp. 74-75.
3. Ibid., p. 75.

Chapter 3 — Battle Plan of Containment
1. Oxford English Dictionary, 2nd Ed., Vol. XII, Clarendon Press, Oxford 1989, p. 568-569.
2. The World Fact Book, United States Central Intelligence Agency, Washington, DC 20505, 1992, p. 365.
3. Pastor Randel McCarty, sermon notes, Cathedral of Praise Assembly of God, Cordova, TN, 18 July 1994.

Chapter 4 — New World Order
1. *The Rise of the House of Rothschild* by Egon Ceasar, Western Islands, Belmont, MA, 1972, p. 8.

2. Bastiat, p. 10.

3. William F. Jasper, *Global Tyranny Step by Step* (Appleton, WI: Western Islands Publishers, 1992), p. 281.

4. John Maynard Keynes, *The Economic Consequences of the Peace*, 1st ed. 1919, reprint 1920) [*The Collected Writings of John Maynard Keynes*, Vol. II, The Economic Consequences of the Peace, McMillan/St. Martins Press, for the Royal Economic Society, London, this ed. 1971, p. 148-149.]

5. *Webster's New World Dictionary*, Third College Edition.

6. *The Rise of the House of Rothschild* by Egon Ceasar, conte Western Islands, Belmont, MA, 1972, p. 8.

7. Milton Friedman, *Newsweek*, May 2, 1983, "More Double Talk at the Fed," p. 72.

8. Congressman Louis T. McFadden on the Federal Reserve Corporation remarks in Congress as quoted in *The Federal Reserve Hoax* by Wickliffe B. Vennard, Boston, Forum Publication Company, 1934, p. 89.

9. *Human Development Report of the Economic and Social Council of the United Nations*, June 1994, p. 84.

10. Rowan Gaither, president of the Ford Foundation, statement made during conversation with Norman Dodd, research director for a special committee to investigate tax-exempted foundations, U.S. House of Representatives, December 1953, quoted in a letter dated Dec. 29, 1962, from Norman Dodd to Dr. Howard E. Kershner of the Christian Freedom Foundation, 250 West 57th Street, New York, NY.

11. Antony C. Sutton, *America's Secret Establishment* (Billings, MT: Liberty House Press, 1986), p. 4.

12. Ibid., p. 172.

13. Cable News Network, evening news prior to Operation Desert Storm.

Chapter 5 — Implementation of the New World Order

1. Theme coined by Clinton confidante and campaign advisor James Carville during the presidential campaign of 1992.
2. Parenthetical material after each of the items below is my emphasis.
3. Donald McAlvany, *McAlvany Intelligence Advisor*, April 1993, pp. 1-2.
4. Federal Register, Executive Orders of the President, U.S. Government. Quoted in *Unravelling the New World Order*. March 1994, FAMC, Inc., 3500 JFK Parkway, Ft. Collins, CO 80525, p. 3.
5. Joann Bruso, *Colorado Christian News*, February 1994.

Chapter 6 — Age of Disinformation

1. *Webster's New World Dictionary of American English*, Third College Edition.
2. Federal Reserve Governor Wayne Angell quoted in *Monetary and Economic Review*, Special Report on Disinformation, FAMC, Inc., 3500 JFK Pkwy, Fort Collins, CO 80525, May 1991, p. 3.
3. Testimony before the House Banking Committee, following stock market crash October 1987.
4. Statement of Alan Greenspan at the Dallas Airport, 19 October 1987, before press microphones as the stock market was collapsing, reported on the wire services.
5. Wire service reports.
6. Bastiat, pp. 9-10.
7. Ibid, p. 10.
8. Mark Memmot, *USA Today*, 25 July 1994, "U.S. Budget Turns Surplus," p. 2B.
9. "Face the Nation," CBS News, 24 July 1994.

Chapter 7 — Mysteries of Commercial Babylon

1. Alfred Fraser Tyler, quoted in *Monetary and Economic Review*, FAMC, Inc., 3500 JFK Pkwy, Fort Collins, CO 80525, January 1992, p. 6.
2. *Mein Kampf* by Adolph Hitler, Reynal & Hitchcock, New York 1941, p. 56-57.
3. *Webster's New World Dictionary*, Third College Edition.
4. *Webster's New World Dictionary*, Third College Edition.

Chapter 8 — Partners in Crime

1. *Webster's New World Dictionary*, Third College Edition.
2. Carroll Quigley, *Tragedy and Hope, A History of the World in Our Time* (New York: McMillan and Co., 1966).
3. General Douglas MacArthur quoted in *Monetary and Economic Review*, FAMC, Inc., 3500 JFK Parkway, Fort Collins, CO 80525, December 1993, p. 6.
4. *Study on Health Care in America*, National Center for Policy Analysis, Washington, D.C., p. 56 of the Health Care Briefing Book for Congressional Candidates.
5. R.E. McMaster, *The Reaper*, June 8, 1994, p. 6.
6. *Monthly Statement of the Public Debt of the United States*, Bureau of the Public Debt, Department of the Treasury, 31 May 1994.
7. *Webster's New World Dictionary*, Third College Edition.

Chapter 9 — The Heart of Power

1. *Congressional Record*, 30 September 1941.
2. *Billions for the Bankers*, updated fourth edition, J.A. Thauberger, Regina, Saskatchewan S4P2Z6, p. 28-29.
3. *The New Encyclopedia Britannica*, Vol. 9, fifteenth edition, p. 995, Encyclopedia Britannica, Inc., Chicago.

4. Andrew Jackson, Veto Message, National Banking Act, July 1832. Quoted by Thomas F. Gordon, *The Bank of the United States*. New York: Bert Franklin, 1967, p. 118.

5. Robert W. Lee, *Conservative Digest*, November 1985, p.43-48, quoting B.C. Forbes in *Current Opinion*, December 1960.

6. J.A. Thauberger, *Billions for the Bankers*. Published by J.A. Thauberger, Regina, Saskatchewan, Canada S4P2Z6, updated fourth edition, p. 21.

7. Karl Marx, *Manifesto of the Communist Party*, London, 1848, Plank Number Five.

8. Thauberger, p. 15-16.

Chapter 10 — Storm Clouds of Disorder

1. "Social and Technological Forecasts for the Next Twenty-five Years," World Future Society, Bethesda, MD, p. 1.

2. Werner, Richard, Oxford University, Oxford, England. Quoted in *Monetary and Economic Review*, FAMC, Inc., 3500 JFK Parkway, Fort Collins, CO 80525, July 1993, p. 7.

3. International Mass Retailing Association/Age Wave, 1994 Study.

4. John Waggoner, *USA Today*, "Mutual Fund Losses Anger Novice Investors" 16 June 1994, p. B-1.

5. Ibid.

6. Paul Wright, "Planned Pension Panic," *Monetary and Economic Review*, January 1994, p. 1.

7. James R. Healey, "Derivatives Again Cost Paine Webber," *USA Today*, 25 July 1994, p. B-1.

8. Testimony by William Seidman before the U.S. House of Representatives Budget Committee, Feb. 7, 1991.

9. Thomas Jefferson, quoted in *The Story of Our Money*, second edition, by Olive Cushing Dwinell. Boston: Forum Pub-

lishing Co., 1946, p. 84.
10. "With Debt Burgeoning, Could the U.S. Default?" by Kathleen Day, *Washington Post*, 14 June 1992, p. H-1.
11. Ibid.
12. Ibid.

Chapter 11 — Financial Privacy and the Cashless Society
1. William Wood, *Denver Post*, "As World Turns: Experts Foresee 300-plus Countries" 30 Aug. 1992, p. 19A.
2. Julian Minghi, *Denver Post*, 30 Aug. 1992, p. 23A.
3. Charles E. Bates, "Government 'Peeping Toms': Closing the Government Peephole." *Monetary and Economic Review*, Nov. 1993, p. 1.
4. Norman N. Franz, "New World Order, Phase II: The New Political Order, Part 2," *Unravelling the New World Order*, Apr. 1994, p. 7.
5. Norman N. Franz, "New World Order, Phase II" *Unravelling the New World Order*, April 1994, p. 7.
6. Ibid.

Chapter 12 — Wealth Transfer and Asset Allocation
1. John Evans, "Currency Trading Hits New Heights," *The European*, 13-19 May 1994, #209, p. 1.

Chapter 13 — The Joseph Generation
1. Pastor Randel McCarty, sermon notes, Cathedral of Praise Assembly of God, Cordova, TN, 17 July 1994.

Free Bank and Insurance Company Analysis!

Yes! I accept your offer for the book and the challenge to become one of few Americans who understands how knowledge of the system can help me avoid the effects of the coming economic disorder.

Please send me additional information regarding:
(please check as many as you are interested in)

❑ *Unravelling The New World Order* subscription details
❑ *Monetary and Economic Review* subscription details
❑ Information on "storm-proofing" my assets
❑ Information on your next seminar
❑ Information on your economic projections
❑ FAMC's catalog of additional recommended educational materials
❑ Information on a free bank and insurance company analysis (please include name, city and state of your bank and insurance company).

Name: _____

Address: _____

City, State, Zip: _____

Phone: (_____) _____

Detach and mail today! Send to:

Publication Department
FAMC, Inc.
3500 JFK Parkway
Fort Collins, Colorado 80525
(800) 336-7000

Or, for faster service, you may FAX your order to (303) 223-4996.